THE DESCENT
OF GOD

THE DESCENT OF GOD

Divine Suffering in History and Theology

JOSEPH M. HALLMAN

Fortress Press   *Minneapolis*

THE DESCENT OF GOD
Divine Suffering in History and Theology

Scripture quotations unless otherwise noted are from the Revised Standard Version of the Bible, copyright © 1946, 1952, and 1971 by the Division of Christian Education of the National Council of Churches.

Cover design by Patricia Boman
Book design by Karen Buck
Author photo by Tatha Wiley

Library of Congress Cataloging-in-Publication Data

Hallman, Joseph M., 1939–
    The descent of God : divine suffering in history and theology /
Joseph M. Hallman.
        p.   cm.
    Includes bibliographical references and index.
    ISBN 0-8006-2485-8
    1. Suffering of God—History of doctrines.   2. God—Immutability—
History of doctrines.   I. Title.
BT153.S8H34   1991
231'.4—dc20   91-4086
                                                                         CIP

The paper used in this publication meets the minimum requirements of American National Standard for Information Sciences—Permanence of Paper for Printed Library Materials, ANSI Z329.48-1984.   ∞™

Manufactured in the U.S.A.   AF 1-2485

93   92   91   1   2   3   4   5   6   7   8   9   10

To the members of my adventurous family,
both past and present.

CONTENTS

ABBREVIATIONS

ACW   *Ancient Christian Writers,* Westminster, Md.: Newman.

ANF   *Ante-Nicene Fathers,* New York: Charles Scribner's Sons.

CCL   *Corpus Christianorum. Series Latina,* Turnholt: Brepols.

CSEL *Corpus Scriptorum Ecclesiasticorum Latinorum,* Vienna.

GCS   *Die griechischen christlichen Schriftsteller der ersten drei Jahrhunderte,* Berlin: Akademie-Verlag.

GNO   *Gregorii Nysseni Opera,* Werner Jaeger, ed. (Leiden: Brill, 1952f.).

NPNF *Nicene and Post-Nicene Fathers,* Grand Rapids, Mich.: Eerdmans.

PG   Migne, *Patrologia, series graeca,* Paris.

PL   Migne, *Patrologia, series latina,* Paris.

SC   *Sources chretiennes,* Paris: Editions du Cerf.

PREFACE

"Have this mind among yourselves, which is yours in Christ Jesus, who, though he was in the form of God, did not count equality with God a thing to be grasped, but emptied himself, taking the form of a servant, being born in the likeness of men. And being found in human form he humbled himself and became obedient unto death, even death on a cross." Phil. 2:5–8.

"In the beginning was the Word, and the Word was with God, and the Word was God. . . . And the Word became flesh and dwelt among us, full of grace and truth; we have beheld his glory, glory as of the only Son from the Father." John 1:1 and 14.

The prologue of John's Gospel and Phil. 2:5–11 present an important feature of the Christian understanding of God as well as one that is difficult to express in rational terms. The statements that the divine Word became flesh and dwelled among us and that God emptied out divinity in Jesus and took on the form of a slave seem contradictory. How could God become human while remaining God? These difficult passages suggest that Jesus was more than a prophet, more than even the greatest of them. Jesus was God. In response to Arianism during the fourth century, the Christian tradition absorbed in a dogmatic way the "high" Christology implied in these and similar texts. Many theologians today think that this high Christology, especially in its doctrinal formulation from 325–381, is problematic or even objectionable either because of its presumed mythological roots or because of the philosophical conceptuality of the dogmas. On both grounds conciliar Christology seems irrelevant to contemporary Christian faith's concern for perfecting the human, especially in the areas of social and economic justice and world peace.

There is another way to read these christological texts and the view of God which they present, a way that is rooted in the tradition itself in a minority of writers. In spite of the fact that their philosophical presuppositions would indicate otherwise, several, beginning with Philo of Alexandria (c. 30 B.C.E.–45 C.E.), attempted to adhere to the portrait of the biblical deity as one who suffers and changes.

I discovered much of the material for this book either by accident, as in the case of Tertullian (160–240), or by perusing scholarly footnotes, as in the case of Pseudo-Didymus the Blind (late fourth century). I contend that several texts from the early tradition diverge from the mainstream on the question of divine impassibility and immutability. The predominance of the view among early Christian authors as well as contemporary historians of theology that God is immutable and impassible has caused divergent formulations suggesting the opposite to go unnoticed.

The historical study (chaps. 2 through 5) begins with Philo of Alexandria in the first century and ends with St. Augustine, who died early in the fifth. Philo's understanding of divine immutability is examined through his treatise on the subject. The Christian thinkers who followed him, especially Clement of Alexandria (150–215), Origen (185–254), and the author of a work entitled *Ad Theopompum* (third century), showed that although they absorb the philosophical view of divine impassibility and immutability, they departed from it in various ways.

Chapter 3 shows how both Tertullian and Lactantius (240–320) questioned the prevailing middle Platonic teaching about God by arguing that God has emotions and does change. Novatian and especially Arnobius (early fourth century) denied it.

Chapter 4 considers Athanasius (295–373), Gregory of Nyssa (330–395), and the author of a late fourth century commentary on the Psalms discovered at Tura and shows how their belief in the

Incarnate Logos influenced their philosophical commitment to divine immutability. Athanasius resisted the Arian logic of divine immutability, while Gregory contributed a positive notion of infinity on the divine and mutability on the temporal level. To the author of the commentary, belief that the Word was made flesh and truly lived in Jesus of Nazareth meant that in some way God actually changed and suffered for us in him. On the heterodox side, we will examine a recent theory that at the heart of Arianism is a theology of divine suffering, and that this explains the lowering of the Logos to the level of a primordial creature.

Chapter 5 contends that both Hilary of Poitiers (d. 367) and Augustine (354–430) saw Christian belief in the Incarnation as a challenge to the prevailing philosophical understanding of God. Although neither was able to formulate this systematically, nevertheless, especially for Augustine, the Incarnation was a revelation that God became humble, something that philosophers could never discover.

The book concludes with a discussion of God and change in two major modern philosophers, Hegel and Whitehead. They grasped in a metaphysical way, and each quite differently, that Christian belief necessitates a substantial revision in the understanding of God. By Hegel's time the Enlightenment and the reaction of the Christian churches had already eliminated all possibility for radical metaphysical revision within the formal boundaries of Christian theology. Hegel's system, however, was deeply influenced by his belief in incarnation. Although Whitehead was not a theologian, he had more than a nominal adherence to the Christian message. It implicitly pervades his work. Hegel and Whitehead are Christian thinkers who grasp on the philosophical level what Christianity teaches: that God is present in the midst of temporal physical existence.

In light of modern attempts to ascribe change and suffering to God, conciliar Christology may be recovered today. If it is possible to conceive divine perfection as perfection in change, the dogmas of the fourth century may live again in an important although unexpected way. Hegel and Whitehead offer new possibilities for reconceptualizing incarnational Christology. Because they are able to argue that God changes and suffers while remaining perfect, they may allow us to express more coherently how Christian belief in the Incarnation leads to a unique understanding of the God of Christian faith.

Christians need not ascend to the divine because God has already descended to the human. No matter how influential the teachings of Platonism have been among Christian theologians, mystics, and ascetics, the Christian journey is essentially different from that which ancient philosophers traveled. Hegel and Whitehead, responding in different ways to the challenge of modernity, recovered this side of the Christian story in their view of God. For them we move forward with the divine rather than upward toward it.

—Joseph M. Hallman

ACKNOWLEDGMENTS

I wish to acknowledge my mentor and friend, Robert L. Wilken of the University of Virginia, who read this manuscript in an earlier version. He advised me many years ago to combine the study of early Christian theology with process thought. The support of my family has been of the utmost importance, that of my friend and spouse Janice Ray, my sons David and Eric, and my daughter Sara. I also want to thank John McDonough, Paul Duff, Jeff Carlson, Bob Zeidel, Winston Chrislock, Bob Rush, Joe Laker, Walter and Rose Renn, Jud Shaver, Zelinda Fouant, Gale Yee, Eileen Michels, and Jeanne Neff, who supported my efforts in many different and important ways.

Several grants from both Wheeling Jesuit College and the University of St. Thomas made this book possible, as well as a sabbatical from each institution.

As far as texts and translations of the material in Greek, I used the volumes of the *Loeb Classical Library* where possible. These have Greek and English on opposite pages, thus are user-friendly for those who (a) have facility in Greek but want to read quickly; (b) have, like this author, less facility in Greek but can use the Greek to check the English; (c) know no Greek at all, which might be the reader's situation. Otherwise I used the best text available, whether Greek or Latin, even though this involved changing rapidly from one edition to another. I hope the reader will not be confused by these changes, and will be able to follow my argument in the light of the texts. Finally, I attempted to use recent English translations (which I cite in the footnotes). I also noted when I made my own translation. Otherwise, I used ANF or NPNF for these.

For transliteration of Greek I followed the substitutions listed in *The Journal of Biblical Literature* 107 (1988): 583 with one addition. In cases where a *gamma* precedes a *kappa* I substituted *n* for the *gamma*.

Portions of chapters 2, 3, and 5 have appeared in scholarly journals—namely, *Recherches de Théologie ancienne et médiévale, The Second Century,* and *Theological Studies.* I am grateful to them for allowing me to use those particular studies within the larger argument of this work.

1

INCARNATION AS A POETIC FICTION
The Philosophers

Greek philosophy was always "in search of something which persisted through all change."[1] Socrates could accept his unjust condemnation and death because he was convinced that he had discovered the unchanging. He expected to enjoy it through his soul in life after death. To exempt the divine from change Aristotle concluded God was a mind which "thinks only of thinking" and of nothing else, all else being mutable. For Plotinus the soul which is unhappily attached to the body is able to discover the unchanging One by passing into the true sanctuary wherein the alone meets the alone.

Anaximander (c. 610–540 B.C.E.) says flatly, "the all is unchangeable."[2] Anaxagoras (c. 500–428) in Aristotle's *Physics* describes the ultimate as the impassible mind.[3] The atoms of Democritus (fifth century) are impassible[4] and immutable.[5]

---

[1] John Burnet, *Early Greek Philosophy,* 4th ed. (London: Adam and Charles Black, 1930), 9. See also G. Watson, "The Problem of the Unchanging in Greek Philosophy," *Neue Zeitschrift für Systematische Theologie und Religionsphilosophie* 27 (1985): 57–70.

[2] *to de pan ametablēton einai.* Hermann Diels, *Die Fragmente der Vorsokratiker,* 12 ed. by Walter Kranz (Zurich: Weidmann, 1966–67), vol. 1, p. 81, line 10.

[3] *ton noun apathē.* ibid., vol. 2, p. 20, line 34; also p. 29, line 31.

[4] *apathēs.* ibid., vol. 2, p. 114, line 13.

[5] *analloiōta.* ibid., vol. 2, p. 84, line 15. See also 97,24; 98,36; 99.4; 94,20.

Xenophanes (sixth century),[6] Melissos (fifth century),[7] and An-
tiphones the Sophist (also fifth century) express this theme in
various forms.[8]

Plato (c. 429–347 B.C.E.) analyzes the relation between perfection and change somewhat differently in the middle dialogues, the *Republic, Phaedo,* and *Symposium,* than in the later
Timaeus.[9] He begins by strongly asserting that the divine is unchangeable and impassible and develops that view considerably
in the *Timaeus.*

In the *Symposium* Diotima tells Socrates that love is neither
god nor mortal, but a great daimon. It is less than divine because
it lacks the beautiful and the good, which it desires.[10] That which
lacks beauty and goodness desires them, and is therefore not a
god. The discovery of the beautiful in a vision of "eternal being,
neither becoming nor perishing, neither increasing nor diminishing" is the final object of love. Beauty does not exist in anything else, but in "singularity of form independent by itself."
All things coming to be and perishing partake in it, yet the
beautiful becomes neither greater nor less and is affected by
nothing.[11] One must ascend "on the rungs of a ladder . . . from
bodily beauty . . . to beautiful deeds, from deeds to beautiful
learning, and from learning at last to that particular study which
is concerned with the beautiful itself and that alone; so that in
the end he comes to know the very essence of beauty."[12]

Once one has beheld the divine beauty, the vision remains
and only then does true virtue become possible.[13] The last section of the *Symposium,* which features the confession of the ho-
mosexual love of the drunken Alcibiades for Socrates, places this
vision of perfect beauty in comic relief. Love itself should always

---

[6] Ibid., vol. 1, 124.7–8; 123.18; 121,32.

[7] Ibid., vol. 1, 267,9; 258,18.

[8] Ibid., vol. 2, 339,15.

[9] Leonard J. Eslick, "Plato as Dipolar Theist," *Process Studies* 12, no. 4 (Winter
1982): 247.

[10] 202 D–E. Plato in twelve volumes, *Loeb Classical Library* (Cambridge:
Harvard University Press, 1967–84) is used throughout this section.

[11] Ibid., 210E–211B.

[12] Ibid., 211C.

[13] Ibid., 212A.

be honored for the sake of imperishable beauty, its ultimate object, something far removed from the grasp of Alcibiades, at least for the moment.

The *Phaedo* contains some of Plato's strongest language about the main impediment in the search for beauty: the body. It is a hindrance that contaminates the soul, keeping it from finding truth.[14] The fact of our recollected knowledge demonstrates that souls existed in a timeless realm before their entry into bodies.[15]

True being is always the same. Socrates asks, "Absolute equality, absolute beauty, any absolute existence, true being— do they ever admit of any change whatsoever? Or does each absolute essence, since it is uniform and exists by itself, remain the same and never in any way admit of any change?" Cebes replies that they must of necessity remain the same.[16] The realm of the soul is the pure, everlasting, immortal, and changeless.[17] Reincarnation is the fate of those who have not freed themselves from the influences of the body,[18] and evil is the soul's belief that the sense objects that please or pain it are distinctive and true; this belief completely bonds evil to the body.[19] Whatever is beautiful is beautiful because of its participation in absolute beauty.[20] The *Phaedo* ends with the heroic and beautiful death of Socrates, an illustration of the doctrine of the soul's imperishability. The soul of Socrates will presumably return to its original spiritual home among the absolutes, no longer polluted by the body and its influences.

The discussion of God in the *Republic* is in the context of Plato's critique of the stories of gods and goddesses in the Homeric epics. It extends his discussion of eternal being even further, and situates it in the context of Greek religion. In Book 2 Plato argues that since God does only good, the cause for evil should be sought elsewhere. In spite of Homer's statements, Zeus does

---

[14] Ibid., 66A–67A.
[15] Ibid., 75C–76E.
[16] Ibid., 78D.
[17] Ibid., 79D.
[18] Ibid., 81E.
[19] Ibid., 83C–D.
[20] Ibid., 100C.

not arbitrarily allot good and evil.[21] The belief that God unjustly allots good and evil is not only false but harmful to the republic.

Plato then develops his understanding of divine immutability. To be altered (*alloioutai*) and moved (*kineitai*) by another happens least to the best things; the soul, for example, is less affected by external states of affairs than the body. Since God is the best, God is least alterable by another.[22] If God decided to alter the divine state, it must be for the worse; since God is not deficient in anything, God could not change for the better. This leads to the following corollary: "No poet then . . . must be allowed to tell us that 'The gods, in the likeness of strangers, many disguises assume as they visit the cities of mortals.'"[23]

On the basis of the absolute immutability of the divine, Plato effectively denies the truth of the stories of incarnation expressed in the Homeric epics. If the divine is immutable, the form assumed by a god must be a disguise, thus a false representation.[24] Real incarnation is impossible.

The heart of Plato's critique of religion in the *Republic* is his insistence that the mimetic narration proper to the poet, upon which religion is based, is essentially immoral. Because poetry imitates something real, it only appears to be true. It evokes strong feelings from the audience, nonetheless, and stories of the unworthy actions of the gods and goddesses give young people false ideas. Zeus cannot truly be overcome with desire (*epithumia*) for Hera because gods cannot experience desire. And the poetic description of the afterlife is unattractive; since it cannot edify those who must face death as warriors, it should be repressed.[25] Plato favors only straightforward, first-person narration by a poet.[26]

Book 10 of the *Republic* returns to this earlier discussion. Mimesis is viewed as a corruption of the mind of all those who

---

[21] Ibid., 379D.
[22] Ibid., 380E–381A.
[23] Ibid., 381D.
[24] *Laws* 10.894; *Phil.* 33B & C.
[25] *Republic* 3. 386A.
[26] Ibid., 3. 392D–394B.

do not understand its true nature.[27] "What is mimesis?" Plato asks. Because of his reverence for Homer, he hesitates to speak negatively about it;[28] he answers the question by appealing to the theory of forms and uses painting as an example. God creates the form of a couch, the carpenter builds it according to the form, but the painter who paints a picture of the couch is merely an imitator. The painter does what Homer did,[29] which is to imitate only the appearance of things and remain three steps away from truth.[30] Mimesis is a form of play, not to be taken seriously in the sober republic.[31]

Plato then ponders the power that mimesis has over us. Why does it work? Why are we led to participate as audiences in third-rate truth? He associates mimesis with that part of us which is remote from intelligence.[32] His most important charge is that mimesis is a corrupting influence: to our detriment we identify unintelligently with the emotions of characters in epics and plays. We should, therefore, allow no real poetry into the city, only hymns to the gods and praises of good men. Poets should be banished.[33]

Unlike poets, philosophers apprehend the eternal and the true, having knowledge of that essence which does not wander between becoming and perishing.[34] The idea of the good is the cause of knowledge,[35] and of all that is right and beautiful, the source of truth and reason.[36] This theory of truth leads to Plato's negative judgment about poets and mimesis. The stories of the gods and goddesses are dangerous, and third-rate poetic imitations can be seriously misleading.

Such is the story that a god can visit human beings in human guise. Because God cannot change, divine visitation simply

---

[27] Ibid., 10. 595B.
[28] Ibid.
[29] Ibid., 597E.
[30] Ibid., 601B.
[31] Ibid., 602B.
[32] Ibid., 603B.
[33] Ibid., 605B–607A.
[34] Ibid., 6. 485B.
[35] Ibid., 7. 508E.
[36] Ibid., 7. 517C.

cannot occur. Plato's critique of religious stories, mimesis, and belief in incarnation arises directly from the impassibility and immutability of the divine. If God cannot change or be affected, the stories are false and the poetry that teaches them harmful. The idea of the immutability of being is developed further, however, in the *Sophist*.[37] In that work, being is power (*dunamis*) producing a change or being affected by a cause. As described by the Stranger,

> Everything which possesses any power of any kind, either to produce a change in anything of any nature or to be affected even in the least degree by the slightest cause, though it be only on one occasion, has real existence. For I set up as a definition which defines being, that it is nothing else than power.[38]

The discussants try to choose between Heraclitus ("All things are in motion") and Parmenides ("All things are at rest") but find it impossible. They reject the idea that motion applies only to the bodily realm and not to being. Theaetetus calls it "shocking" to say that motion, life, soul, and mind are not present to universal being so that it neither lives nor thinks, but exists in awful holiness, immovable, and without mind. It seems equally absurd to say that being does have mind and soul, but that it is *akinēton*, immovable.[39] Eventually they "resolve" the question by constructing five categories, two of which are motion and rest.

Important to our purpose is that Plato is willing to modify his notion of immutability in favor of the quite different understanding of being as the power to affect and to be affected by another. This is a relational conception of being which, had it been developed, would have led to a quite different understanding of God.

The *Timaeus* was one of the most important dialogues for early as well as medieval Christian writers. In contrast to the *Phaedo*, it is positive about the world of change. Prior notes,

---

[37] The *Sophist* may well have been written after the *Timaeus*, but this does not affect my analysis. See William J. Prior, *Unity and Development in Plato's Metaphysics* (LaSalle, Ill.: Open Court, 1985), Introduction and Appendix, for discussion of the chronology of Plato's works.

[38] *Sophist* 247E.

[39] Ibid., 248E–249A.

"Earlier disparagement of the phenomenal world is largely absent from this dialogue. . . . The cosmos is now a suitable object for serious philosophical study."[40] The discourse on creation begins with the following question: "What is that which eternally exists and has no becoming, and what is that which eternally becomes, which never has being?"[41] The first can be known with the help of reason since it is eternally, but the second is known only by opinion (*doxa*) because it is an object of sensation, and it becomes and perishes, and never really is.[42] Plato then argues that all things that become, need a cause. The objects of sensation become and perish, therefore they are caused. Yet "to discover the maker and father of all is indeed a task and to declare to all what one discovers is impossible."[43]

The cosmos is a copy or an image of an eternal paradigm that is a living creature. The copy becomes, the paradigm is.[44] As being is to becoming, so is truth to belief.[45] Thus in the world of change we cannot always achieve truth but must settle for belief, because we are dealing with the copies of things rather than with the very paradigms used by the Creator.

Out of divine goodness, the Creator takes the disorganized visible things and organizes them, placing reason within the soul of the cosmos, then the soul in the cosmic body. Plato's extremely complex account proceeds to explain how everything came to be, including directions, geometric shapes, numbers, fire, earth, water, air, stars, birds, fish, land animals, and the human race. The deities of Homer are also generated and told to complete the work of creation.[46]

Eventually Plato introduces yet another form to explain the origin of things. This form is "baffling and obscure. What essential property, then, are we to conceive it to possess? This in particular, that it should be the receptacle, and as it were the

---

[40] William J. Prior, *Unity and Development*, 92.
[41] *Timaeus*, 27C.
[42] Ibid., 27D–28A.
[43] Ibid., 28C.
[44] Ibid., 29B; 30C–D; 37D.
[45] Ibid., 29C.
[46] Ibid., 41A.

nurse of all becoming." The receptacle is a substance that receives all changing things, locates them, and supports their underlying reality as they change. Plato calls it a divine mother, an invisible and unshaped image partaking of the intelligible in some way. The Creator is the father, the creation the offspring.[47]

A shift of great importance occurred here, and one that, unlike the teaching on the relation between divine perfection and immutability, influenced the Christian understanding of God and creation very little. In the *Timaeus*, receptivity is a necessary general cosmological component introduced to explain how things can become other things while continuing to remain in existence. Another noticeable shift is that Plato is much less critical of the reality of the deities than in the *Republic*. In fact, the demiurge generates them, then gives each their various tasks in completing the particulars of creation.[48] Whereas the *Republic* demythologizes, the *Timaeus* remythologizes.

Plato is obviously not a theist in the Jewish and Christian sense, and he certainly always held to the anti-Homeric anti-incarnational principle that the divine cannot visit the human realm. Yet to explain the creation of the cosmos he saw the need to add the notion of the receptacle and a remythologized understanding of the deities, even though the divine is absolutely immutable. His final comments on change occur in an analysis in *Laws* 10 of ten kinds of motion, the highest of which is self-movement. Whatever moves itself is alive and has a soul.[49] Other kinds include circular motion, locomotion, combination, separation, increase, decrease, becoming, perishing, and being moved by another. Nevertheless a thing really exists only when it remains the same; when it changes it is destroyed.[50] The idea of relational being which is presented in the *Sophist* and of the motherly receptacle in the *Timaeus* are ultimately displaced in favor of the equation of perfect existence with absolute immutability.

---

[47] Ibid., 50C–D. See Prior, *Unity and Development*, 108ff. for a description of the receptacle and how it fits into the development of Plato's metaphysics as a whole.

[48] *Timaeus*, 40E–41A.

[49] *Laws*, 893B–904E; also *Phaedrus*, 245C–246A.

[50] *Laws*, 894A.

ARISTOTLE

In his *On the Heavens* Aristotle (384–322 B.C.E.) describes the existence of a primary body that is eternal, unbegotten, immortal, without growth or change of quality, ageless, and impassible.[51] The plurality of heavenly beings is also described as *analloiōta kai apathē*, unchanging and impassible.[52] His analysis of motion takes up where Plato's left off, and it is a full-fledged philosophy of change. Repeatedly, sometimes tortuously, Aristotle attempts to understand the various types as well as the basic character of motion. For him "the one thing above all that needed explanation" was "the phenomenon of motion and change."[53]

The *Physics* eventually concludes that motion or *kinēsis* must be restricted to only three types of change. This disallows generating and perishing, which are not called movements, but transformations or *metabolai*. Aristotle devotes an entire treatise to the discussion of these two transformations, which is entitled *On Coming to Be and Perishing*. These *metabolai* are changes of substance, whereas the three types of *kinēsis* are of quantity (increase or decrease), quality, and spatial movement.[54]

Aristotle formally classifies quality as having four types in *Categories* 9B, 32–33. First, there are habits and dispositions. Habits are more lasting, and include the virtues and knowledge; dispositions include heat, cold, disease, health, and so on. Second, there are inborn capacities and incapacities, such as athletic abilities or lack thereof. Third, there are affective qualities such as sweetness, bitterness, sourness, coldness, warmth, whiteness, blackness; in the soul are found temper, madness, and irascibility. Finally, there are shape and form: straight, crooked, triangular, and so forth. Various examples of qualitative change or *alloiōsis*

---

[51] 270A ff. Aristotle in twenty-three volumes, *Loeb Classical Library* (Cambridge: Harvard University Press, 1963–1983).

[52] Ibid., 279A.

[53] W. K. C. Guthrie, *The Greek Philosophers from Thales to Aristotle* (New York: Harper, 1975), 128.

[54] See Aristotle, *Physics,* 192B; 200B; 224A; 225B–226B; 241A; 243A; 244B–248A; *Metaphysics,* 1069B; 1088A. Plato (*Theaetetus,* 181C) had already distinguished between *alloiōsis* and *kinēsis.* Aristotle maintained this distinction. The first referred to a change of quality and the latter to spatial motion.

which are scattered throughout Aristotle's corpus apparently fit into these classes, including color;[55] state of health;[56] sweetness, density, or dryness;[57] and change resulting from sensations, or passive change (*alloiōsis kata to pathos*).[58]

In *Categories* Aristotle states that an *alloiōsis* can occur without any other kind of change: "For what changes as to an affection does not necessarily increase or diminish—and likewise with the others. Thus *alloiōsis* would be distinct from the other changes."[59] We shall see later how a fourth-century Christian author argues that a specific *alloiōsis* involving no other type of change occurs in God in the Incarnation.

Book Lamda of the *Metaphysics* is the most important source for Aristotle's theology. In it he argues that to explain the continuous eternal motion of the cosmos there must be a substance that is both unmoved (*akinētos*) and eternal. Since actuality precedes potentiality, it must also be actual. Besides being unmoved and eternal, God is thought, life, happiness, and good.[60] But considering God to be thought or mind causes some difficulty:

> If mind thinks nothing, where is its dignity? It is in just the same state as a man who is asleep. If it thinks, but something else determines its thinking, then since that which is its essence is not thinking but potentiality, it cannot be the best reality, because it derives its excellence from the act of thinking.[61]

Aristotle draws the following conclusion about God: "Therefore mind thinks itself, if it is that which is best; and its thinking is a thinking of thinking."[62]

It is important to see whether and how the various types of change apply to God. The argument from motion, constructed as it is on the basis of cosmic movement, seems to exempt God from only one form of *kinēsis*, that of movement in space. This is

---

[55] *Phys.*, 201A,6.
[56] Ibid., 224A,30.
[57] Ibid., 244B,6.
[58] *Categories*, 15A,22; *Phys.*, 246A, 2–3; *Metaphys.*, 1069B,12; 1088A,32; *Peri Psychē*, 416B,34.
[59] *Categ.*, 14.15A.13.
[60] *Metaphys.*, 1072B; Aristotle also argues for an unmoved mover in *Phys.*, 8.
[61] *Metaphys.*, 1074B.
[62] *estin Hē noēsis noēseos noēsis*.

not Aristotle's conclusion, however. The unmoved mover is also impassible and immutable, *apathes kai analloiōton:* "For all other kinds of motion are posterior to spatial motion. Thus it is clear why this substance has these attributes."[63] But is it clear? Aristotle has certainly not demonstrated it here. He assumes that all forms of change depend upon local motion. Hence if a substance is exempt from movement in space, it can change neither qualitatively nor quantitatively. And the unmoved mover, functioning eternally in the cosmos, had not come to be and can certainly not pass out of existence.

The Christian author of a commentary on the Psalms will take issue with Aristotle, arguing that a change of quality in God can occur, and for Christian faith does so in the descent of the Word made flesh. In the midst of the discussion of God as unmoved mover, Aristotle decries the myths about the gods visiting us in human form as "unintelligible."[64]

STOICS AND MIDDLE PLATONISTS

In contrast to Plato's and Aristotle's conceptions of the divine, that of the Stoics, because of their monism and materialism, held little attraction for Christian thinkers, except perhaps for Tertullian. According to Zeno (born c. 490 B.C.E.) there were two ultimate principles, God and matter. God is the active force in nature, the *logos* is its providence and natural order; matter is passive and without qualities; the human soul emanates from the supreme divine *logos* and is the source of human rationality. One of the favorite descriptions of the Stoic deity is spirit or breath (*pneuma*), which pervades the entire world.[65] Because of this strong sense of divine immanence, the Stoics were accused of teaching a mutable deity by thinkers such as Plutarch and Origen.[66] Their ethical teaching was much more influential

---

[63] *Metaphys.,* 1073A.

[64] Ibid., 1074B.

[65] See Joannes Ab Arnim, *Stoicorum Veterum Fragmenta* (Dubuque: Brown Reprint Library, n.d., 1:24; 2:299–313.

[66] Ibid., 2:309–11.

among Christian writers, however, and it is on this basis that *apatheia* came to be attributed to the divine as a perfection, especially in Clement of Alexandria.[67]

Attribution of immutability to God in Christianity came mainly through the influence of Middle Platonism, especially from Philo of Alexandria, whom we will discuss in the next chapter.[68] A certain philosopher named Celsus is a good example of a Middle Platonist who held this view. He attacked Christianity around 178–180 C.E. in a work entitled *Alethēs logos* or *The True Word*, which is now preserved in Origen's refutation.[69]

Part of Celsus's critique concerned his belief that Christians had introduced mutability and passibility into the divine because of their teaching of incarnation. His comments are crucial to this book, because they show that at least one Middle Platonic philosopher, who was not a Christian, saw that the Christian story had reintroduced into Greek philosophical tradition what Celsus considered a false and outmoded element, that a god could visit the human race. Origen attempted to refute that charge but without giving up the idea of the Incarnation of the deity in Jesus of Nazareth.

---

[67] See Theodor Rüther, *Die sittliche forderung der apatheia in den beiden ersten christlichen Jahrhunderten und bei Klemens von Alexandrien* (Freiburg: Herder, 1949), chap. 1. See also P. de Labriolle, "Apatheia" in *Melanges de philologie de litterature et d'histoire anciennes offerts à A. Ernout* (Paris: C. Klinsieck, 1940): 215–25; M. Spanneut, *La stoicisme des Peres de Clement de Rome a Clement d'Alexandrie* (Paris: Editions du Seuil, 1957); *Permanence du Stoicisme de Zénon a Malraux* (Gembloux: J. Ducolot, 1973); J. Stelzenberger, *Die Beziehungen der früchristlichen Sittenlehre zur Ethik der Stoa* (München: Max Hüber, 1933); J. M. Rist, *The Stoics* (Berkeley: University of California Press, 1978).

[68] See John Dillon, *The Middle Platonists: A Study of Platonism 80 B.C.–A.D. 220* (London: Duckworth, 1977); W. Pannenberg, "The Appropriation of the Philosophical Concept of God as a Dogmatic Problem of Christian Theology," in *Basic Questions in Theology* (Philadelphia: Fortress, 1971), vol. 2: 119–83; C. Andresen, "Justin und der mittlere Platonismus," *Zeitschrift für die Neutestamentliche Wissenschaft* 44(1952–53): 157–95; *Logos und Nomos: Die Polemik des Kelson wider des Christentum* (Berlin: W. de Gruyter, 1955); R. A. Norris, *God and World in Early Christian Theology* (New York: Seabury, 1965). Philo never attributes *apatheia* to God, however.

[69] The best Greek edition of the *Contra Celsum* is in vol. 1 and 2 of the GCS. Here I will refer to the English translation by Henry Chadwick, *Origen: Contra Celsum* (Cambridge: University Press, 1953) and will give page numbers from this translation in parentheses.

Celsus interpreted belief in the Incarnation as a lapse into the old myths. As Plato had put it, "No poet . . . must be allowed to tell us that 'the gods in the likeness of strangers, many disguises assume as they visit the cities of mortals.'"[70] Celsus argued that he had nothing new to say about the divine, and was only repeating ancient doctrines.[71]

> God is good and beautiful and happy, and exists in the most beautiful state. If then He comes down to men, He must undergo change, a change from good to bad, from beautiful to shameful, from happiness to misfortune, and from what is best to what is most wicked. Who would undergo a change like this? It is the nature only of a mortal being to undergo change and remoulding, whereas it is the nature of an immortal being to remain the same without alteration. Accordingly, God could not be capable of undergoing this change.[72]

Origen replies that although indeed God does descend in providence and concern for human affairs, the divine essence remains unchanged. On this last point he cites Ps. 101 (102):28 and Mal. 3:6, two classic texts.[73] Unlike the gods of Epicurus and the Stoics, the Christian God does not change. He does descend, however. A close reading of the *Contra Celsum* confirms that Origen accepted Plato's description of the divine while rejecting Plato's objection to the divine descent. We will see that Augustine did something similar with Plotinus. Origen writes:

> He who came down to men was originally "in the form of God" and because of his love to men "emptied himself" that men might be able to receive him. But he underwent no change from good to bad; for "he did no sin"; nor from beautiful to shameful, for "he knew no sin." Nor did he pass from happiness to misfortune; although "he humbled himself," nevertheless he was happy, even when he humbled himself in the way expedient for our race.[74]

---

[70] Plato, *Republic* 381D. Celsus's description of God below is at least partially dependent on 381B and C.

[71] The relevant section is in *Contra Celsum* 4. 14–19.

[72] *Contra Celsum* 4.15 (192–93).

[73] See the discussion at the end of this chapter.

[74] *Contra Celsum* 4.15 (193).

Origen uses the example of a physician who sees terrible things and touches wounds, yet does not contract the diseases of the sick:

> The Word remains Word in essence. He suffers nothing of the experience of the body or the soul. But sometimes he comes down to the level of him who is unable to look upon the radiance and brilliance of the Deity, and becomes, as it were, flesh.[75]

Because Celsus does not understand Christian Scriptures, he does not grasp "how because of his great love to man, God made one special descent in order to convert those whom the divine scriptures mystically calls 'the lost sheep of the house of Israel.'"[76] Notice how Origen writes "one special descent" to distinguish Christian belief from the Homeric mythology of many visitations. Celsus's final comment presents an either/or: "Either God really does change, as they say, into a mortal body; and it has already been said that this is an impossibility. Or He does not change, but makes those who see Him think He does so, and leads them astray and tells lies."[77]

Origen replies that the Word changes in the perception of each person according to his or her spiritual need, but does not change in essence. Neither does the soul of Jesus change essentially. Nevertheless, the descent really occurred. Origen cites again the kenotic passage from Philippians. He then accepts the fact that those who saw Jesus may not have recognized him as the Word, but they were "deceived" for their own good. The Word accepted this limited condition for the sake of our salvation.[78]

PLOTINUS

Plotinus (c. 205–269/270 C.E.) was Origen's contemporary and later became one of Augustine's main philosophical resources.

---

[75] Ibid., (194).
[76] Ibid., 4.17 (195).
[77] Ibid., 4.18 (195).
[78] Ibid., 4.19 (196–97).

Although difficult to gauge its influence on Christian theology, Plotinus taught a trinity of three divine hypostases. In a descending hierarchy they are the One (or Good or Beauty), Mind, and Soul.[79] By means of this speculative structure, he attempts to synthesize the theological work of previous philosophers, such as Plato, Aristotle, the Stoics, and the Middle Platonists.

The One is beyond being, mind, thought, or soul.[80] Intellect or Mind is the repository of the intelligible forms; and the lowest hypostasis, Soul, infuses the changing world with life.[81] Matter is evil because it is without form, so evil is the privation of form.[82] Although bodiliness is not evil (because it is a form), for Plotinus it is precisely the embodied human condition that creates the problem of human existence: how to free the soul from its dependence on the body and the external environment.

In his treatise on Beauty, which is reminiscent of Socrates' speech in the *Symposium*, Plotinus describes the ascent of the soul to the Beautiful. To ascend to the higher world we must strip off what we put on in our descent until we are able to see with the self alone:

> If anyone sees it, what passion will he feel, what longing in his desire to be united with it, what a shock of delight! . . . He who has seen it glories in its beauty and is full of wonder and delight, enduring a shock which causes no hurt, loving with true passion and piercing longing.[83]

Once we experience absolute beauty we need none of its lower forms. "The man who attains this is blessed in seeing that blessed sight, and he who fails to attain it has failed utterly." The beauty one sees in bodies is but an image, a trace, or a shadow of the absolute. It is like a reflection on water and if one mistakes it for

---

[79] *Ennead* 1.2; 2.9; 6.9. Plotinus, *Loeb Classical Library* (Cambridge: Harvard University Press, 1966–88). Rist argues that although Plotinus is not completely clear on their relationship, the Good is higher than the Beautiful. That problem is too complicated for discussion in this context, however. See J. M. Rist, *Plotinus: The Road to Reality* (Cambridge: University Press, 1967), 53ff.

[80] *Ennead*, 1.7.

[81] Ibid., 1.2; 6.9.8–9.

[82] Ibid., 1.11; also 3.6.11.13.

[83] Ibid., 1.6.7.

the real thing and clings to it, one drowns.[84] To attain the absolute one must develop an inner sight that moves away from bodily and spiritual instances of beauty and ascends to the absolute by means of the soul.

Plotinus describes three vocations, that of philosopher, musician, and lover, and how one is able to move upward differently in these different journeys toward absolute beauty.[85] Here he also depends upon the ascent imagery of the *Symposium*. The philosopher is closer to beauty than the musician and lover, but the latter two ascend by means of harmony and rhythm, or beautiful bodies, laws, or souls that one admires.

One of the more graphic images of how we relate to the One is that of a chorus surrounding a leader who never moves. As we allow ourselves to turn our attention to the leader rather than to external distractions, we learn to sing correctly. We form a choric ballet around the One.[86] In this ballet the soul sees the source of life, of mind, the principle of being, the cause of good, the root of love. Once the soul attains to full contemplation, she truly thinks, is impassible, truly lives.[87] She passes beyond the statues in the temple into the sanctuary itself. Ultimately it is the flight of the alone to the alone.[88] Plotinus holds that nothing spiritual, whether the Good, Mind, or Soul, is capable of being changed or affected by another. To be nonbodily is to be *atrepton* and *apathēs* by nature, unchanging and impassible.[89] Being is not impassible because it is isolated, but because it is being. It is completely sufficient unto itself. Yet from the human experience of emotion and learning, the soul certainly seems mutable and passible. Plotinus goes to great lengths to show that what seems to be is simply not the case.

Admittedly the soul feels pleasure and pain, anger, envy, jealousy, and desire. It is always moved and changed.[90] In spite

---

[84] Ibid., 1.6.8.
[85] Ibid., 1.3.
[86] Ibid., 6.9.8.
[87] Ibid., 6.9.9.14–15.
[88] Ibid., 6.9.11.51.
[89] Ibid., 3.6.
[90] Ibid., *kinoumenēs kai metaballousēs.*

of the appearance of passing from potentiality to actuality, however, there is no *alloiōsis* or *pathos* for the soul, which always remains the same in its substratum and essence.[91] Virtues and vices do not constitute changes of the soul.[92] Plotinus faces the objection that if the soul is impassible by nature, then why do we need to make it so?[93] The answer is that the soul is asleep and needs to be purified in order to recover its true impassible nature: "For the activity of sense-perception is that of the soul asleep . . . but the true wakening is a getting up from the body, not with the body. Getting up with the body is only getting out of one sleep into another; but the true rising is a rising altogether away from bodies."[94]

Ideal well-being comes from living at a distance from the cares and concerns of the world. The highest end of human life is to live unperturbed by poverty, war, sickness, slavery, and death in complete impassibility.[95]

In another text Plotinus distinguishes between two souls, a higher one that is unchangeable and impassible, and a lower soul that is mixed with the body.[96] The higher soul uses the body and lower soul as a tool, but it itself is "free from all responsibility for the evils that man does and suffers; these concern the living being, the joint self."[97] The true soul is at peace, "turning to itself and resting in itself. The changes and clamor in us come from what is attached to us and from the affections of the joint entity." Virtues and vices belong to the lower soul, as do reincarnation and punishment in Hades.[98] The higher soul does not suffer with the body. Its impassibility is in imitation of the Good. It ought not share in the feelings of the lower soul, which is its inferior companion.[99]

---

[91] Ibid., 3.6.1.34ff.
[92] Ibid., 3.6.3. For his reflections on change and the categories of Aristotle, see 6.1–3.
[93] Ibid., 3.6.5.
[94] Ibid., 3.6.69–76.
[95] Ibid., 1.4.
[96] Ibid., 1.1.2.
[97] Ibid., 1.1.9.
[98] Ibid., 1.1.10–12.
[99] Ibid., 1.2.5–6.

Plotinus's view of the world of change and suffering is decidedly negative. In spite of this he criticizes the Gnostics for holding that material existence is evil in and of itself.[100] The study of Plotinus led Augustine away from Manichean pessimism. Yet in the developing theology of Christianity, Plotinus's understanding of God needed a radical transformation.

From the fourth century on, christological reflection directed the Christian use of philosophy. The Arians rejected the divinity of the Word of God because of belief in the Incarnation. This is not difficult to imagine given the classic understanding of immutability and the sensitivity of Arians to the issue of divine suffering. The contrary affirmation of the divinity of the Word caused Athanasius and other "orthodox" to begin to question, at least to a small degree, the classic understanding of God's immutability. If God has truly shared this world, especially its human aspect, God can no longer be seen as immutably distant. The changing world becomes the dwelling place for the divine.

SCRIPTURE

The opening pages of the Bible set the tone: God creates first the world, then the human race, male and female, in the divine image. The startling anthropomorphic images of Genesis 2 teach that God is present and concerned for humanity—the garden, the helpmate, the naming of the animals. Yet there is also the divine law—the tree of the knowledge of good and evil, and human freedom to sin. Sin leads to fratricide, then judgment and the Flood. The possibility of repentance and redemption is constant. Redemption is a change of the divine will, a reversal of condemnation resulting from God's compassion overcoming divine justice. These images of God are deeply rooted everywhere in the Scriptures. The renewal of the covenant after the Flood, the exodus and the Law of Moses, the conquest, the rise and fall of the Kings, the fall and restoration of Israel—this is a story of

---

[100] Ibid., 2.9.

divine immersion in the affairs of God's people and in human history in general.

The message of the prophets, especially Hosea, Amos, Jeremiah, and Ezekiel, is that God indeed does change, has feelings, and suffers for the sake of Israel.[101] Even the exalted God of the Priestly tradition is deeply involved in the affairs of the world, as is the God of the other three authors of the Pentateuch. Psalms and Wisdom literature are no exception. In Job, for example, God is real enough, sympathetic enough, and eventually near enough to answer Job's questions.

Jesus proclaims God's responsive presence in the world. God is *Abba*, Father. Although Jesus and John the Baptizer strongly express God's impending judgment of wrath, the parables of the Good Samaritan and the Prodigal Son direct us to the concrete reality of divine love and forgiveness in ways that subvert our rational views of friendship and justice. The hymnic rhythms of God's incarnation and descent originate in the very beginning of Christianity and are found in Paul and John.

The kenotic image of Jesus in the hymn of Phil. 2:5–11 became extremely influential in theology, as we will see. Jesus preexists in a divine status but takes on the form of a slave to become human.[102] John's prologue (1:14) makes the powerful assertion that the divine Word became flesh, which in his Gospel expresses the full identity of Jesus of Nazareth. But the statement is problematic. In the words of C. K. Barrett, "It is difficult to determine precisely the meaning of *egeneto* (became). It cannot mean 'became,' since the Word continues to be the subject of further statements."[103] In other words, for Barrett, it is a simple

---

[101] See especially Abraham Heschel, *The Prophets,* 2 vols. (New York: Harper, 1976).

[102] R. P. Martin, *Carmen Christi: Philippians ii.5–11 in Recent Interpretation and in the Setting of Early Christian Worship* (Cambridge: University Press, 1967); also his appended note in *Philippians: The New Century Bible Commentary* (Grand Rapids: Eerdmans, 1976) 109–116; for a solid, recent, and eloquent interpretation see Fred B. Craddock, *Philippians* (Atlanta: John Knox, 1985), 39–43.

[103] C. K. Barrett, *The Gospel according to John: An Introduction with Commentary and Notes on the Greek Text,* 2nd ed. (Philadelphia: Westminster, 1978); see also Rudolf Bultmann, *The Gospel of John: A Commentary* (Philadelphia: Westminster, 1971), 60–83.

question of either/or. Either the Word became flesh, that is, stopped being divine, or it did not become at all.

In spite of this problem, it was only a matter of time before theologians, especially Athanasius, realized the great power of this symbol to express the nearness of God. The author of the fourth Gospel retells the entire story of Jesus in its light, and eventually the Synoptics come to be read, at least in Alexandria, through his eyes. Once full attention turns toward the Incarnation in the fourth century, this reading becomes dogmatized. God suffers with us and for us in this man Jesus, although we cannot say precisely how this is the case.

IMMUTABILITY PROOF TEXTS

Everyone familiar with modern biblical studies knows that the philosophical doctrines of divine immutability and impassibility are not taught in the Bible. The writers did not reflect on the divine nature from a metaphysical perspective. Nevertheless, early Christian thinkers found several scriptural texts that they used to support divine immutability or impassibility. The text used most often for this purpose is Exod. 3:14, where God reveals the divine name as YHWH. It appears with striking regularity as the passage that identifies the God of Scripture with the God of Greek philosophy. Although the meaning of the Hebrew word is debatable, it certainly does not refer to the *to on*, being-itself, of Greek philosophy.[104]

Two texts in particular seem to support divine immutability, Mal. 3:6 and Ps. 102:18. The first begins bluntly: "For I the Lord do not change" (*lō' sānîtî*). The second section of the passage explains the sense of this assertion: since Yahweh does not change the divine will for the survival of Israel, it will survive its present catastrophe. "Ever since the days of your ancestors you have turned aside from my statutes and have not kept them. Return to me, and I will return to you" (v. 7). These last words certainly

---

[104] See "YHWH" in G. Botterweck and H. Ringgren, *Theological Dictionary of the Old Testament* (Grand Rapids: Eerdmans, 1986), 5: 500–521.

imply change on God's part, a change by which God returns Israel to its fortunes. Although the Lord does not change the divine will that Israel survive, this passage shows no reflection of absolute immutability in the philosophical sense.

Ps. 102:6–7 compares God's way of being with that of the world. God's everlastingness is unlike the perishability of all else: "They will perish, but you endure; they will all wear out like a garment. You change them like clothing, and they pass away (*weyahalipu*); but you are the same, and your years have no end."[105]

Sirach 42:16–21 invites philosophical reflection. God is omniscient, "knows all that may be known" (v. 18); "discloses what has been and what is to be" (v. 19); "no thought escapes him, and nothing is hidden from him" (v. 20). God is also everlasting and in need of no one (v. 21). Here too the context is a contrast with creation and, although it is not drawn as sharply as in Psalm 102, it suggests itself in v. 23. In both passages, God's changelessness refers to divine imperishability, not immutability in the philosophical sense.

Although the later writings of the New Testament show the influence of philosophical conceptions of God, this influence is quite weak.[106] Hebrews 6:17 calls God's promise and oath unchangeable. It is important to notice that this is the only instance of the philosophical term *ametatheton* in the entire New Testament, and that it does not refer directly to God but to the divine oath and promise.

On the other hand, James 1:17 does describe God's unchanging nature, although the text itself suggests its unphilosophical character. God is "Father of lights, with whom there is no variation

---

[105] Cited in Heb.1:11–12; See E. Jacob, "Le Dieu souffrant, un thème théologique vétérotestamentaire," *Zeitschrift für die altestamentliche Wissenschaft* 95(1983): 1.

[106] In several Pauline texts, God is invisible and incorruptible, such as Rom.1:20; 1 Tim.1:17; Hebr.11:27. Col.1:14 has *eikōn tou theou ton aoraton*. In 1 Tim.6:16 God is the only one having *athanasia*. Both passages from 1 Tim. may be hymnic in structure. *Athanasia* and *aphtharsia* are Pauline terms usually designating the risen body. See 1 Cor.15:53; 42; 50; 54. For other usage of *aphtharsia* see K. Aland, *Vollständige Konkordanz Zum Griechischen Neuen Testament* (Berlin: Walter de Gruyter, 1983), 1: 147.

or shadow due to change."[107] Divine invariance here contrasts
with planetary movements, which vary from season to season,
and night to day. The visibility of planetary light is temporary. The
creator of the planets is distinctive, because the "Father of lights" is
not subject to the changes in creation. Unlike the movement of the
planets, God is constant.

In spite of the various passages that were used to support
a philosophic view of divine immutability, the Bible does not,
strictly speaking, support only that view. This is not to argue that
the theological tradition deliberately misinterpreted these biblical
texts, but only to suggest that another understanding of God might
legitimately be held today, one that allows a more literal interpretation of those biblical passages that testify to the reality of divine
emotion, change, love for and even descent to the human race.

---

[107] *Patros tōn phōtōn par' hō ouk eni parallagē hē tropēs aposkiasma.*

2

ATHENS OR JERUSALEM?
The Alexandrian Response

Philo of Alexandria (c. 30 B.C.E.–45 C.E.), a contemporary of Jesus, was the single most important resource for early Christian philosophical reflection on God's nature. Because he was strongly committed to both Hellenistic philosophy and to the Bible, he attempted to reconcile them when they seemed to conflict. His religious beliefs and practices as a Jew would then become philosophically defensible in the cultural idiom of his day. Philo set the stage for the many apologetic attempts by Christian writers to effect this reconciliation. Above all he provided the groundwork for their christological use of the Logos idea, which became so influential in the development of Christian trinitarian thought.[1]

The attempt to reconcile the Greek notion of immutable, perfect divine being with belief in the God of Abraham, Isaac, and Jacob came originally from Philo. Most importantly, his is the very first monograph on God's immutability, the *Quod deus immutabilis sit.* Before discussing this treatise, we should note something about Philo's terminology which has hitherto gone unnoticed. In spite of his adherence to the Hellenistic understanding that

---

[1] J. N. D. Kelly, *Early Christian Doctrines,* rev. ed. (San Francisco: Harper & Row, 1978), 7–11.

God is impassible and without emotion,[2] not once in his entire
corpus did Philo connect the technical term *apathēs* or *apatheia*
to God. And although he held that God is immutable, he never
used the term *analloiōtos* to express this. An argument from
terminological omission is admittedly weak, but there is clear
philosophical precedent for the use of these two terms to describe God, especially the latter. Why did Philo not conform to
this usage? Is it possible that in spite of such precedent, the use
of *apatheia* in connection with the God of Jewish faith was
improper in a way unknown to philosophy? And even though
Philo rejected the literal sense of various anthropomorphic passages, would this description of the God of Israel have been too
extreme?[3]

The *Quod deus sit immutabilis* is obviously the second part of
a commentary on Gen. 6:1–12. It discusses vv. 4b–12. Of special
importance for us is Philo's discussion of Gen. 6:6–7:

> And the Lord was sorry that he had made humankind on the earth,
> and it grieved him to his heart. So the Lord said, "I will blot out
> from the earth the human beings I have created—people together
> with animals and creeping things and birds of the air, for I am
> sorry that I have made them."[4]

Philo knew that on the basis of this passage some believe that
the Creator repented the creation of the human race. Philo described as "godless" all who literally interpreted Gen. 6:5–7. "For
what greater impiety could there be than to suppose that the
Unchanging changes?"[5] Even the soul of the Sage achieves a

---

[2] For example, see the *De Abrahamo,* 202.

[3] Robert M. Grant hints at this in *The Early Christian Doctrine of God* (Char-
lottesville: University of Virginia Press, 1966), 29, n. 43.

[4] Philo, *Loeb Classical Library* (Cambridge: Harvard University Press, 1968),
vol. 3. For Gen. 6:6 (or 6:7) Philo read "God took it to heart" (*enethymēthē*). The
Hebrew text states that God repented (*wayyinnāḥem*). For 6:7 (6:8) he read "was
displeased that he made them" (*ethymōthēn*). In *Questiones et Solutiones in Gen-
esin* 1.95 he calls this last statement about God an "exaggeration." For comparison among various Greek manuscripts and the Hebrew text in passages such as
these, see Charles T. Fritsch, *The Anti-Anthropomorphisms of the Greek Pentateuch*
(Princeton: University Press, 1943).

[5] *Quod deus immutabilis sit,* 22: *ton atrepton trepesthai.*

certain quietude, and if such peace can be found among human beings, can we "doubt that He, the Imperishable Blessed One who has taken as His own the sovereignty of the virtues, of perfection itself and beatitude, knows no change of will, but ever holds fast to what He proposed from the first, without any alteration?"[6]

Two examples of human mutability follow. They are instructive because they indicate in a compelling way the type of change which Philo means to deny to God. He is not just repeating Platonic phrases but analyzing how divine immutability applies specifically to the God of the Bible. First is the human experience of the loss of friends. We tire of our friends and turn from them, "though we have no charge to bring against them, and count them among our enemies or at best as strangers."[7] God has "no such fickleness." God never wavers in love.

Second, Philo cites the human phenomenon of peer pressure or conformity. We change our judgments to conform to those of others "who have not remained constant."[8] This mutability of judgment is morally reprehensible because it is based on fear of what others think. God feels no peer pressure and is not a conformist. God knows all because God created all, and lives in the fullness of eternity. Philo's two examples express the religious insight that grounds his conception of divine immutability. Both forms of change, loss of a friend through neglect and conforming because of peer pressure, are impossible for God, who is our constant companion and is unwavering in will. Notice that Philo tells us concretely what type of change he denies of God. He is not necessarily denying any and all types of mutability and passibility.

After describing the levels of God's creation, Philo turns to Gen. 6:7, which reads: "So the Lord said, 'I will blot out from the earth the human beings I have created—people together with animals and creeping things and birds of the air, for I am sorry that I have made them.'" Philo writes, "Some on hearing these

---

[6] Ibid., 26.
[7] Ibid., 27–28.
[8] Ibid., 28.

words supposed that the Existent feels wrath and anger." God "is
not susceptible to any passion at all. For disquiet is peculiar to
human weakness."[9] Then why does Scripture ascribe these emotions to God? Christian authors will use Philo's answer tirelessly.
These expressions are a kind of "elementary lesson to admonish
those who could not otherwise be brought to their senses."[10] They
are only pedagogical in nature, not literally true. Philo mentions
other biblical anthropomorphisms and their pedagogical value.
In teaching God's anger, jealousy, and wrath, the Bible is similar
to surgeons who withhold the truth from someone who needs to
have a limb amputated.[11] If Scripture represents God as "dealing
in threats, indignation and anger," or again "as using weapons
of war for His onslaughts on the unrighteous," it is to admonish
the fool.[12]

In this context the contradiction between Num. 23:19 ("God
is not as a man") and Deut. 8:5 ("like a man He shall train his
son") becomes a hermeneutical problem. The idea that God has
emotions comes from a comparison with human nature. Exactly
how valid is this comparison? Numbers 23:19 gives a better description of God than Deut. 8:5, which is merely for purposes of
instructing the many.

In another place Philo states that Num. 23:19 is true, implying that Deut. 8:5 is not.[13] The first passage applies to those who
love God, the second to those inferior believers who only fear
God. For Philo a God who is "like a man" is a God who is angry,
threatens, and punishes. These two texts commonly appear in
similar opposition in Philo. Num. 23:19 "keeps truth in view"
while Deut. 8:5 is for "duller folk," whom God will chasten.[14]
To describe God as a human is for our feeble comprehension. In
reality God is unbegotten, deathless, unchanging, holy, alone

[9] For wrath, anger, and disquiet, *thymois, orgais, astheneias.*
[10] *Quod deus,* 52.
[11] Ibid., 66.
[12] Ibid., 68.
[13] *Quest. et Solut. in Gen.,* 2.54.
[14] *Legum Allegoriae,* 2.33.

blessed.[15] God swears an oath in Exod. 13:11. Does God need to make oaths to guarantee their truth? No! "God is not as man." To give God human passions (*anthrōpopathes*) is impious. Parts and passions cannot belong to God. The oath of God is a crutch for our weakness.

Philo finally returns to Gen. 6:7, arguing that it attributes wrath only metaphorically to God.[16] He is grateful that the passage does not have a different word order, since it would then suggest divine repentance, something impossible for the "all-foreseeing nature of God."[17]

In summary, for this treatise God is *atreptos* and without human emotions. Expressions that indicate that God is angry are pedagogical because God is immutable. Philo commonly uses *atreptos*, literally, "non-turning," for God's immutability. He uses *ametablētos* (not being overthrown) less often. Never, as mentioned previously, does he use *analloiōtos*.[18] Indeed *atreptos* can even be attained by souls who share it with God.[19]

Philo describes this sharing in *De posteritate Caini*, 1–31. The soul is like a ship at the mercy of a stormy sea. But "proximity to a stable object (God) produces a desire to be like it and a longing for peace."[20] God is stable (*aklinēs*), and creation is unstable. Abraham drew near to God and attained stability. "For a truly unchanging soul has access to the unchanging God."[21] The

---

[15] *agenētou, aphthartou, atreptou, hagiou, monon makariou. De Sacrificiis Abelis et Caini*, 101. For a discussion of the difference between Greek and Jewish responses to anthropomorphisms as well as the importance of Num. 23:19 for Philo, see H. A. Wolfson, *Philo* (Cambridge: Harvard University Press, 1948), 2:127ff.

[16] *Quod deus*, 70.

[17] The different and more problematic word order is *dioti epoiēsa autous, ethymōthēn*.

[18] Philo uses *analloiōtos* only once in *De somniis*, 1.188 to describe the Platonic world of ideas. The following are the important texts to consult here: *Leg. All.*, 2.89; *De somniis*, 1:232, 249; 2:221, 228, 237; *De mutatione nominum*, 46, 54, 87; *De Specialibus Legibus*, 1:312; *De confusione linguarum*, 96; *De cherubim*, 90; *Quest. et solut. in Exodum*, 2.37; *Quest. et solut. in Gen.*, 1.42.

[19] *De somniis*, 2.228, 237.

[20] *De posteritate Caini*, 23.

[21] Ibid., 27. The quality of *atreptos* belongs primarily to God, but also to the Logos, then to the Sages, finally to the person who makes gradual progress. See also *De somniis* 2.237.

words of Deut. 5:31 addressed to Moses ("But you, stand here by me") contain a double affirmation: First, God moves and turns all but does not change; second, He "makes the worthy man sharer of His own nature, which is repose."[22]

Further on, however, Philo shows that he is sensitive to the idea of divine descent. God is said to "go down" with his people (Gen. 46:4) and bring them up while not moving from place to place. Although immutable, God initiates the act whereby God's people can find repose in the unchanging:

> But with those who go down in the sense of changing their place . . . I will go down, in all-pervading Presence without any alteration of locality. . . . I do this in pity for rational nature, that it may be caused to rise out of the nether world of the passions . . . guided step by step by Me.[23]

There is no departure from the understanding that God is *to on* in this text, but there is an obvious suggestion that a divine descent occurs in which God shares the divine immutability out of pity for human persons.

In *De plantatione* Philo offers a similar thought. In spite of an invective against anthropomorphisms and anthropopathisms in this work,[24] as well as a long discussion of how God "obtains a portion" although needing nothing,[25] Philo makes the surprising statement that "in so far as He is Ruler, He has both powers, both to bestow benefits and to inflict evil, changing His dealing as the recompense due to the doer of every deed demands."[26] Does this type of change conflict with divine immutability? The biblical doctrine of divine moral constancy implies God's ability to respond to changing circumstances of reward or punishment. The biblical doctrine of divine responsiveness has broken through

---

[22] *De post. Caini,* 28. God is *akinēton te kai atrepton.*

[23] Ibid., 30–31.

[24] *De plantatione,* esp. 35.

[25] Ibid., 54–72.

[26] Ibid., 87.

Philo's philosophical insistence that God cannot change God's will because all is foreknown.

Philo also states occasionally that God shows anger and mercy,[27] and at times writes quite realistically about divine happiness.[28] Brehier's entire discussion of God in Philo revolves around the question of the abstract philosophic description of God as opposed to a concrete biblical understanding.[29] Sandmel argues that God as *to on* is distinct from God as *Theos* or *Kyrios* in Philo, *to on* being unknowable as such, *Theos* and *Kyrios* corresponding to God as creator and governor of the world.[30] Since *atreptos* rather than *analloiōtos* is his favorite philosophical adjective for God's immutability or constancy, and because he has no formal doctrine of divine impassibility, Philo shows that he is aware that the God of Israel cannot be described in language drawn indiscriminately from Greek philosophy. When he applies *atreptos* to the human soul, its meaning for God becomes clear. Although Philo does not say it, *atreptos* is an attribute that might allow for mutability and passibility of some type.

Philo does not, therefore, completely absorb the Greek notion of divine immutability and impassibility. Because his aim is the programatic reconciliation of the Scriptural portrait of God with the Hellenistic notion, he cannot have been expected to see clearly how they might rather fundamentally differ. Nevertheless the Scriptural portrait remained uppermost in his mind.

---

[27] *De vita Mosis,* 1.6; *De somniis,* 2.177f; *De opificio mundi,* 156 in reference to God's response to the sin in the garden.

[28] God's *euphrosynē.* See *De somniis,* 2.177f.

[29] E. Brehier, *Les idees philosophiques et religieuse de Philon D'Alexandrie* (Paris: Librairie Philosophiques J. Vrin, 1950), 69–82; Also R. M. Grant, *The Early Doctrine,* 29 n. 43; 31 n. 47.

[30] Samuel Sandmel, *Philo of Alexandria* (New York: Oxford, 1979), 89–101. For research in Philo up to 1937 see H. L. Goodhart and E. R. Goodenough, "A General Bibliography of Philo Judaeus," in E. R. Goodenough, *The Politics of Philo Judaeus* (New Haven: Yale University Press, 1938), 125–321; from 1937, see R. Radice, *Filone de Alessandria: bibliografia generale 1937–1982* (Napoli: Bibliopolis, 1983); various bibliographic entries during the lifespan of *Studia Philonea,* 6 vols.; for word study see Günther Mayer, *Index Philoneus* (Berlin: Walter de Gruyter, 1974). Also important is the classic study by H. A. Wolfson mentioned above (n. 15) which argues for the prime importance of Philo in the history of philosophical theism.

EARLY CHRISTIAN AUTHORS AND
APOLOGISTS

The earliest Christian writers after the New Testament period
seldom offer systematic reflection on God's nature. Like the New
Testament, this literature is for the most part mixed and unphilosophical. Nevertheless, there is a concern to maintain God's
immutability and impassibility. Clement of Rome's letter *To The
Corinthians* (c. 96 C.E.) argues that God "stands in need of nothing
and desires nothing of anyone except that confession be made to
him."[31] Although Clement does not overtly advocate a technical
doctrine of impassibility, his statement resembles one. This is
actually the biblical idea that purity of heart is superior to sacri-
fice. God clearly does desire something: purity of heart. In another place Clement states that God is free from wrath,[32] but still
warns of an impending condemnation[33] and judgment.[34]

Ignatius of Antioch (martyred between 98–117) is somewhat more theological than the other writers of this period and
has several interesting phrases about Jesus. God is above sea-
sons, timeless, invisible, and cannot suffer.[35] Jesus is our God or
God incarnate[36] who is "first passible and then impassible, Jesus
Christ our Lord."[37] On his way to Rome to be executed Ignatius
fears that his death will be prevented. He writes in the *Letter to
the Romans*:

> What a thrill I shall have from the wild beasts that are ready for
> me! I hope they will make short work of me. I shall coax them on to
> eat me up at once and not to hold off, as sometimes happens,

---

[31] *To the Corinthians* 52.1. For Christian authors in this and the following
chapters, I generally use the standard English translations of Alexander Roberts
and James Donaldson, *The Ante-Nicene Fathers* (New York: Charles Scribner's
Sons, 1926) unless otherwise noted.

[32] Ibid., 19.3: *aorgētos*.

[33] Ibid., 21.

[34] Ibid., 28; 35; 41.

[35] *Pol.* 3,2: *achronon, aoraton, apathē*. See L. W. Barnard, "The Background of
St. Ignatius of Antioch," *Studies in the Apostolic Fathers and their Background* (New
York: Schocken, 1966), chap. 2.

[36] *Eph.* 7,2; 18,2; 19,3; *Eph. inscription; Rom. inscription; Trall.* 7.1.

[37] *Eph.* 7.2.

> through fear. If they are reluctant, I shall force them to it. Forgive
> me—I know what is good for me. Now is the moment I am begin-
> ning to be a disciple.[38]

Ignatius is not suicidal. For him martyrdom is the crown of Christian discipleship; he writes, "Let me imitate the Passion (*pathous*)
of my God."[39] Not only was it important that God suffered in
Jesus. For Ignatius divine suffering provides a paradigm for
Christian martyrdom.

CHRISTIAN APOLOGISTS OF THE
SECOND CENTURY

Justin the Martyr (100–165) became a Christian apologist in the
mid-second century by converting first to Platonism, then to
Christianity. Despite his adherence to the Middle Platonic concept of God, which is, of course, Philo's as well, he shows a strong
concern to maintain the Christian understanding that God is
"a compassionate and long-suffering Father who in Christ has
drawn near to his creation, and who is concerned with the welfare
of every individual soul."[40]

The Christian God is incomprehensible, inexpressible, immutable, impassible, and noncorporal: "For no one may give a
proper name to the ineffable God, and if anyone should dare to say
that there is one, he is hopelessly insane."[41] We may not even properly use the term God, much less Father, Creator, Lord, or Master.[42] Because God is "unchanging," God is "superior to changeable
things."[43] He is "unbegotten and impassible" unlike the pagan

---

[38] 5.2–3. The translation is from Cyril C. Richardson, *Early Christian Fathers*
(New York: Macmillan, 1970), 104–5.

[39] Ibid., 6.3.

[40] L. W. Barnard, *Justin Martyr, His Life and Thought* (London: Cambridge
University Press, 1967), 78.

[41] *1 Apol.* 61.10. For texts and translations of Justin see J. Quasten, *Patrology*
(Westminster, Md.: Newman Press, 1950), 1:201f. For background, especially
Barnard, *Justin Martyr.*

[42] *2 Apol.* 6.

[43] *1 Apol.* 13.4; 20.2.

deities,[44] and Christians can look forward to a future existence that is also impassible.[45] God is too far away from the business of the world to be either named or known.

In spite of this, in text after text, especially in the *Dialogue With Trypho*, Justin's writing impresses its biblical religiosity upon the reader. Most of the argument there does not concern philosophy at all, but the proper interpretation of Jewish Scripture. He becomes most philosophical, and appropriately so, in his apologetic defenses of Christianity to philosophically trained officials. Justin's theological understanding of God is undeveloped in that it does not adequately express his biblical religiosity. As a result, the divine, personal Fatherhood fades into the background. "It was not given to him . . . to unite transcendence and immanence in a system at once rational and biblical."[46]

Aristides' apology (early second century) is an extreme example of the apologetic emphasis on divine transcendence. It is virtually a manual of negative theology.[47] God is incomprehensible, immutable, and impassible, as well as unbegotten, uncreated, and immortal, having no wrath or anger. Since the gods and goddesses of Greece and Rome have these emotional and mutable qualities, they are not divine. They laugh, cry, get angry, are troubled, and have sex. Our God is far above these activities. Aristides sees no way to distinguish the Christian God from pagan deities except by negation. Everything they are, therefore, our God is not.

Athenagoras's *Plea Regarding Christians* (177) transmits Justin's doctrine of a God who is incomprehensible and impassible as well as uncreated, eternal, invisible, and without limit.[48] God is also immortal, immovable and unchangeable.[49]

---

[44] *1 Apol.* 25.2.

[45] *2 Apol.* 1.2; *Dial.* 124.4; 46.7.

[46] Barnard, *Justin Martyr*, 84.

[47] See 1, 4, 5, 7, 10, 13. For the text of Aristides as well as background see J. Geffcken, *Zwei Griechischen Apologeten* (Leipzig and Berlin: Tübner, 1907). English is from ANF 9: 263–79.

[48] *Supplic.* 8 and 10. L. W. Barnard, *Athenagoras: A Study in Second-Century Christian Apologetics* (Paris: Beauchesne, 1972).

[49] *Supplic.* 22: *athanaton kai akinēton kai analloiōton.*

The divine stands in need of nothing: burnt offerings have no effect.[50] Like Aristides, Athanagoras commonly writes about God's immutability and impassibility in polemics against the gods and goddesses. The gods get angry, feel desires, find sacrifices pleasing to them. Our God does none of these things and is therefore superior.[51]

The most striking apologetic passage occurs in the *To Autolycus* of Theophilus (c. 180). In defense of God's anger he writes,

> You will say, then, to me, "Is God angry?" Yes; he is angry with those who act wickedly, but he is good, and kind, and merciful, to those who love and fear him; for he is a chastener of the godless, and father of the righteous; but he is a judge and punisher of the impious.[52]

Immediately afterward Theophilus says, "And he is without beginning, because he is unbegotten, and he is unchangeable (*analloiōtos*) because he is immortal."[53] Later he connects God's immutability to the divine, unoriginate nature: "because he is uncreated, he is also unalterable (*analloiōtos*); so if matter, too, were uncreated, it would be unalterable and equal to God; for that which is created is mutable (*trepton*) and alterable, but that which is uncreated is immutable and unalterable."[54]

Irenaeus's view of God (late second century) is virtually the same. God is uncreated, unbegotten, incomprehensible, without figure, has no beginning or end, is impassible and immutable.[55] The *Adversus Haereses* raises the question of divine impassibility because of the Gnostic creation myth. In his critique of the myth, the impropriety of divine feelings becomes Irenaeus's major theme.

---

[50] *Supplic.* 29; 13; *Res.* 12.

[51] *Supplic.* 21; 22; 29.

[52] *Ad Autol.* 1.3.

[53] Ibid., 1.4.

[54] Ibid., 2.4.

[55] *Adversus Haereses* 2.12.1; 3.8.3; 4.21.3; 4.62; 2.56.1. The citations are from W. W. Harvey, *Sancti Irenaei ep. Lugdunensis libros quinque adversus haereses*, 2 vols. (Cambridge: Typis academicis, 1857). They do not correspond to the numbers used in ANF 1:315f, but the ANF numbers are in Harvey's margin.

According to the myth, the last eon to be produced is Sophia or Wisdom. She is the youngest eon and most distant from the Father, and develops an improper passion to know him. For this offense, according to one version, she is cast out of the pleroma. Then a parthenogenic creation of an amorphous substance occurs which is made out of the solidified emotions resulting from Sophia's ejection. Fear, ignorance, grief, and bewilderment become the matter out of which the world comes to be. Eventually Sophia returns to the pleroma, persuaded that the Father is truly unsearchable.

Irenaeus argues that Sophia could not be in a divine pleroma in the first place if she felt passion.[56] It is a condition for the divinity of the eons that they be impassible. Otherwise they have a substance that is different from God's, that is, material. If they are passible, they are corruptible, and if corruptible, not divine. To the argument that some have feelings and some do not, Irenaeus replies that it is an either/or proposition. Either all the eons are capable of feeling and corruption, or all are not. If they are capable of feeling, they are not divine and the myth is false. Immutability, impassibility, and divinity strictly imply one another.

One passage of special importance in the vast *Adversus Haereses* is the author's description of God as compared to human personality. Irenaeus argues that the Gnostics are self-contradictory because they hold that God is both unknowable and, at the same time, a hierarchy of eons. For Irenaeus these eons are actually human thoughts and feelings hypostasized. If Gnostics construct a mythical divine pleroma out of human thoughts and feelings, Irenaeus contends, they cannot call God unknown. They know God by comparison with themselves. If they knew the truth, however, they would know that God is not like us, and "his thoughts are not like the thoughts of men. For the Father of all is at a vast distance from those affections and passions which operate among men."[57]

---

[56] Ibid., 2.21.4–2.23.
[57] Ibid., 2.15.3.

A list of distinctive divine attributes follows. God is simple, noncomposed, without diverse members. But the eon-less, one God is also total understanding, total spirit, total thought, total intelligence, and total reason, light, and font of all goodness. Irenaeus also states that God is total hearing and total seeing. Not only mental and personal characteristics apply to the one God, but bodily ones as well.[58]

In 2.15.4, which follows immediately, Irenaeus says that God is nevertheless above all these attributes because God is indescribable. Later on he reasserts the fact that God is total seeing and total hearing as well as total intelligence and so forth.[59] For Irenaeus, the Gnostics knew unconsciously that the eons are aspects of human personality. But for Irenaeus they are eternal attributes by which we can speak properly of the one God.[60] Therefore, even though the divine nature is vastly different from ours, we know God by comparing the divine with human personality. If one pursued this line of reasoning, is God not also total receptivity, total sympathy, and total love? Although it is a possible consequence of his argument, Irenaeus does not see this important application.

On the other hand, he believes in the reality of divine wrath and punishment because of biblical teaching. He seems unaware of the problem that this raises given an impassible God, but is content to elucidate the wrath and punishment texts by means of each other.[61] He does give one explanation for divine punishment, however, which is refined later by the Alexandrians. In reference to apostates, he writes, "God does not punish them immediately of himself but . . . punishment falls upon them because they are destitute of all that is good."[62] The crime itself is its own punishment, and God is not directly involved.

---

[58] Robert Grant finds Irenaeus's source in Xenophanes B 24. It reads *oulos horai, oulos de noei, oulos de t'akouei.* See *Gods and the One God* (Philadelphia: Westminster, 1986), 89–90.

[59] *Adv. Haer.* 2.16.4.

[60] Ibid., 2.16.5.

[61] Ibid., 4.44; 4.65.

[62] Ibid., 5.27.2.

CLEMENT OF ALEXANDRIA

Clement (c. 150–215) derives his usual understanding of God
principally from Philo and Middle Platonism, and carries even
further their insistence on the doctrine of divine transcendence.[63]
He holds to divine impassibility with more tenacity than Philo or
any Christian author before him.

In his classic description of transcendence, Clement finds it
necessary to undergo a "purification by confession" in order even
to conceive of God. Only then is one able to attain "contemplation
by analysis, advancing by analysis to the first notion." In a carefully constructed set of assertions, he explains how analysis leads
to a negative description of God. We proceed by

> abstracting from the body its physical properties, taking away the
> dimension of depth, then that of breadth, and then that of length.
> For the point which remains is a unity, so to speak, having posi-
> tion; from which if we abstract position, there is the conception of
> unity.[64]

By casting ourselves into Christ's greatness we are then able
to attain some "conception of the Almighty, knowing not what
He is, but what He is not." God is above space, time, name, and
thought. He is strictly inexpressible and unknowable. "For how
can that be expressed which is neither genus, nor difference, nor
species, nor individual, nor number?"[65] We cannot properly name
that which we do not know. If we call it the One, Good, Mind,
Absolute Being, Father, God, Creator, or Lord, the titles merely
provide support for the mind to keep it from error. None of these

---

[63] See E. F. Osborn, *The Philosophy of Clement of Alexandria*, Texts and Studies, N.S. 3 (New York: Cambridge University Press, 1975), chap. 2; Salvatore
R. C. Lilla, *Clement of Alexandria: A Study in Christian Platonism and Gnosticism*
(London: Oxford University Press, 1971), 213f. Lilla outlines Clement's doctrine
of divine transcendence in seven points showing similarities with Philo, Gnosticism, Plotinus, and Ammonius Saccas.

[64] All references to the *Stromata* and *Paedagogus* are from the edition of
Clement in GCS. I will give volume numbers and pages from this edition in parentheses. *Strom.* 5.12.81, (2:380). On this point in Clement see H. Chadwick's translation of the *Contra Celsum* (Cambridge: University Press, 1965), 429 n. 4.

[65] *Strom.* 5.12.81, (2:380).

titles express God, and all together they are only descriptions of divine power.

For Clement there is no possible analogy between God and the world, because there is no natural relationship.[66] We are not related to God by essence, nature, or power of essence, but only because we are God's work. It is fair to say that for Clement, the human race and the world in general are alien products of God's will, and that this natural alienation provides the backdrop for the divine acts of revelation and salvation. No natural knowledge of God is possible. Clement's insistence on this point highlights the importance for his theology of revelation through the Logos.

In this same passage, the connection between negative theology, impassibility, and divine transcendence is clear. We cannot understand the passions of God by referring to ours; to do this implies an understanding of the Scriptures which is carnal. God is impassible, *apathous*. To suppose that God literally hears anything is impious, "for the Divine Being cannot be declared as it exists." God's biblical joy at our repentance is not truly God's but ours. The prophets appropriate it to God because of our fleshly condition. And God's wrath is, for Clement, "hardly more than a metaphor."[67]

Again and again Clement describes God as completely immutable and impassible, free of anger and without desire.[68] The impassibility of God becomes the model for true Christian virtue. Jesus himself had an impassible human soul, wholly free from human emotions.[69] The Christian Gnostic strives to attain the condition of *apatheia* in imitation of God and of Christ, and this is the essence of true piety.[70]

---

[66] Ibid., 2.16.74–75, (2:152).

[67] R. P. Casey, "Clement of Alexandria and the Beginnings of Christian Platonism," *Harvard Theological Review* 18(1925): 69.

[68] *Strom.* 7.13.16, (3:12); 6.7.60, (2:462); 6.10.80, (2:471); *ECL* 52, (3:151); *Strom.* 4.23.151, (2:315).

[69] *Paedagogus* 1.2.4, (1:91–94). See Theodor Rüther, *Die sittliche Forderung der apatheia* (Freiburg: Herder, 1949) 58–60.

[70] See Osborn, *Philosophy of Clement*, chap. 2; *Strom.* 5.11.67, (2:371); 6.9.71f., (2:467); 7.11.60f., (3:43–44); 7.14.84f., (3:60).

Surprisingly, Clement ascribes passibility to God in some places. His best known text occurs in *Paed.* 1.8.62f., wherein he depicts the Incarnation as an act of love that balances out the divine punishment. Belief in the Incarnation is already challenging the philosophical view of a Christian author, even one who adopts such an extreme understanding of transcendence.

The Lord Teacher sympathized (*sympathēson*) with us because he was embodied and knew our weakness, Clement says, and we ought to see the divine punishment in Scripture in this particular context. Clement also writes of the love felt by both God and the Logos, which we experience in the act of creation. If God is good, how can God be angry and punish? Clement asks. Reproof is the surgery of the soul's passion. The Logos is our great General who punishes to do good, and his censure is a sign of his good will, his chiding is from love. He suffered for us when he might have destroyed us. "For the Divine Being is not angry in the way that some think; but often restrains, and always exhorts humanity, and shows what ought to be done."[71]

God does not feel angry unjustly or out of vengeance but has a loving, saving anger for our benefit. But God does feel anger of some kind, and is therefore not absolutely impassible: "The feeling of anger (if it is proper to call His admonition anger) is full of love for man, God condescending to emotion on man's account; for whose sake also the Word of God became man."[72] How is it possible that God can condescend to the emotion of saving anger? Does the divine condescension out of love imply some form of passibility and mutability? In this remarkable text, Clement does not tell us. Importantly, however, Christian belief in creation and Incarnation becomes a theological instance of divine condescension and the consequent passibility and change on God's part.

There are several other texts where Clement attributes some passibility or emotion to God. When taken as a whole, they indicate a willingness to occasionally modify his insistence on immutability. "Yet the Lord does not weary of admonishing, of

---

[71] (1.133).
[72] Ibid.

terrifying, of exhorting, of arousing, of warning," Clement writes. "No indeed, He awakes men from sleep, and those that have gone astray He causes to rise from out of the darkness itself."[73] Regarding unbelievers, "God is displeased, and them He threatens."[74] Further on, Clement says, "And this dearly loving Father—our true Father never ceases to exhort, to warn, to chasten, to love."[75]

Clement implies that the Incarnate Logos is mutable in a number of texts, such as the following: "So the Savior uses many tones and many devices in working for the salvation of men; His threats are for warning; His rebuke for converting; His lamentation to show pity; His song to encourage."[76] Even more direct is a passage that refers to the indwelling of the Logos. Christians "hear about the image of God, an image which dwells with us, is our counsellor, companion, the sharer of our hearth, which feels with us, feels for us."[77] The following two statements are also noteworthy, given Clement's insistence on divine impassibility:

> Trust, O man, in Him who is man and God; trust O man, in Him who suffered and is adored. Trust, ye slaves, in the living God who was dead.[78]

> The Lord ate from a common bowl, and made the disciples recline on the grass on the ground, and washed their feet, girded with a linen towel—He, the lowly minded God, and Lord of the universe.[79]

Divine impassibility is absolute because of God's absolute transcendence. Coupled with the most extreme statement of God's transcendence in early Christian theology, however, are other texts that show that in some way, even for Clement of Alexandria, God is passible. Whenever he mentions the emotions or passibility of Father and Logos it is obvious that he departs from

---

[73] *Protrepticus* 9.70, (187) in G. W. Butterworth, (trans.), *Clement of Alexandria* (Cambridge: Harvard University Press, 1968), the source of all *Protrep.* references in this book.
[74] *Protrep.* 9.71, (189).
[75] Ibid., 10.75, (205).
[76] Ibid., 4.53, (137).
[77] Ibid.
[78] Ibid., 10.84, (229).
[79] *Paedagogus* 2.3.28.1, (1:179).

the doctrine of absolute divine *apatheia*, which he held more tena-
ciously than anyone before him. Although Origen, like Clement,
also believes that God is impassible, he denies it in one passage
even more strongly than Clement.

ORIGEN OF ALEXANDRIA

The most remarkable text on divine suffering in Origen (c. 185–
254) is in his homily on Ezekiel 6:6. He explicitly denies the
impassibility of God the Father in this homily, as well as that of
the Logos. The savior, Origen says, "descended to earth in pity
for the human race, He suffered our sufferings before he suffered the cross and thought it right to take upon Him our flesh.
For if He had not suffered, He would not have come to take part
in human life. First he suffered then he descended and was
seen." Origen claims here that the Logos suffered in his preexis-
tent condition. He continues:

> What is that passion which He suffered for us? Love is that pas-
> sion. Also the Father Himself and God of the universe, longsuffer-
> ing, very pitying and compassionate, does He not suffer in some
> way? Do you know that when he deals with human things, He
> suffers a human passion? "For the Lord your God endures our ways
> as if a man should endure his son."

In an attempt to correct Philo's negative view of Deut. 8:5, Origen continues:

> Therefore God endures our ways inasmuch as the Son of God bears
> our sufferings. The Father Himself is not impassible. If asked,
> He has pity and compassion, He suffers something of love, and He
> comes to be in those things in which because of the greatness of his
> nature, He cannot share, and for us he endures human sufferings.[80]

---

[80] GCS 8:384–85. This translation is from J. K. Mozeley, *The Impassibility of
God: A Survey of Christian Thought* (Cambridge: University Press, 1926), 60–61.
For Origen, I use the GCS except where indicated otherwise. English for *Peri
Archon* is from G. W. Butterworth, *Origen: On First Principles* (New York: Harper,
1966). For *Contra Celsum* see note 64 above.

All authors agree on the uniqueness of this text. It affirms both the passibility of the Logos even before the Incarnation and, in simple direct language, affirms the passibility of the Father. Disagreement exists, however, on the significance that these statements have. M. Pohlenz sees them as "completely unique" and argues that Origen is only speaking pedagogically.[81] Grant, on the other hand, believes that "something of great theological significance has happened here,"[82] that Origen questioned the doctrine of absolute divine impassibility. Crouzel thinks that Origen is expressing the mysterious paradox by which God is both impassible and passible.[83] Whether or not the words of the homily reflect mere pedagogy, a true rejection of the impassibility of God, or just a passing insight into an aspect of God unseen in other contexts, is not possible to determine. Each of the three possibilities can explain the text equally well, and in fact, Pseudo-Didymus the Blind who was possibly influenced by this teaching of Origen tried to work out a rational understanding of God which preserved both passibility and impassibility, and thereby achieved one of the high points in the Greek patristic understanding of divine suffering.

There are three other instances in which Origen implies divine emotions. *Selecta in Ezekiel* 16:8 simultaneously affirms and denies divine passibility. The strong denial, "God is impassible, just as he is immutable and uncreated," is followed a few lines later by a description of God as one, immutable, and all powerful. Immediately after this, Origen says, "God feels compassion for the one to be pitied; for God is not heartless."[84]

In the *Homily on Numbers* 23:2 Origen strongly portrays the divine emotions of happiness at human conversions and salvation, and sorrow for human sin. It is remarkable, even for a homily, that he depicts the joy of God and of the angels so realistically, and that he cites a great number of biblical passibility texts,

---

[81] *Vom Zorne Gottes: Eine Studie über den Einfluss der griechischen Philosophie auf das alte Christentum* (Göttingen: Vandenhoeck & Ruprecht, 1909), 36.

[82] *The Early Christian Doctrine*, 31.

[83] Henri Crouzel, *Origene et la "conaissance mystique"* (Paris: Desclee de Brower, 1961), 261.

[84] MPG 13.812A: *Sympaschei ho Theos tǭ eleēsai. Ou gar asplagnos ho Theos.*

as though their thematic importance as a whole acutely struck him. Origen seems to be on the verge of a literal interpretation of these texts, but the conclusion to the homily restates his usual theology of divine *apatheia:*

> All those passages in scripture in which God is said to lament, rejoice, hate or be happy are written figuratively and in a human way. It is entirely foreign to the divine nature to have passion or the feeling of mutability, since it endures in unchanged and uninterrupted happiness.[85]

Homily 8.5 on Exodus discusses the divine jealousy of Exod. 10:5. Rather than deny that God feels jealous, Origen explains how jealousy can be conceived in a manner worthy of God: "Here, therefore, God is jealous because he requires and desires that your soul adhere to him; if he seizes you, castigates you, is indignant and angry, and acts jealously toward you, know that he is the hope of your salvation."[86] In this same homily, he previously said: "God does and suffers all things for us that we may be able to learn; he expresses notable and useful affections for us."[87] Unlike the homily on Numbers, there is no denial of passibility. Origen intends to show that God's jealousy is worthy of a God who desires our salvation. His main concern, repeated often in his various discussions of passibility, is to derive interpretations that are worthy of God but responsive to biblical teaching.

Divine Immutability

On the other hand, Origen says very often that the one God cannot suffer or change in any way. Against the Stoics he argues the "unchangeable and unalterable" divine nature[88] and commonly predicates these two attributes of God.[89] The treatise on prayer insists that praying is valuable, even though God is unchangeable

---

[85] GCS 7.211–214.

[86] Ibid., 6.229.

[87] Ibid., 6.227.

[88] *Contra Celsum* (hereafter CC) 1.21, (1:72); 4.14, (1:284); 6.62, (2:132). He finds scriptural basis for this especially in Ps. 101:8 and Mal.3:6.

[89] *Co. John* 6:38, (4:147): *Ho Patēr atreptos kai analloiōtos.*

and foreknows everything.[90] God's nature is such that prayers are eternally foreseen. God is impassible because God is entirely unchangeable: "God's anger is not to be considered a passion. How can an impassible being have a passion? God does not suffer, he is immutable."[91]

Origen's discussions of God's anger occur often in the context of Marcionism, as they did in many early Christian writers. He commonly states that the biblical passages ascribing wrath to God are not literal: "Whenever we read of the anger of God, whether in the Old or the New Testament, we do not take such statements literally, but look for the spiritual meaning in them, endeavoring to understand them in a way that is worthy of God."[92]

God's wrath is not an emotional reaction to a situation, but a method of correction and education, "something he uses in order to correct by stern methods those who have committed many terrible sins."[93] Further in this passage, divine anger is what "each man brings . . . on himself by his sins." Anger is as improper for us as it is for God: "Therefore we do not attribute human passions to God, nor do we hold (other) impious opinions about Him."[94] Origen often discusses divine anger in the context of biblical passages that ascribe unworthy emotions or body parts to God.[95] We ought not to interpret literally any of the texts that mention God's voice, hearing, speech, anger, or repentance.[96] God is not moved by anger or vengeance, and the supposed divine repentance over past decisions is only our changed perspective regarding unchanging divine providence.[97]

---

[90] Chaps. 5–7, (2:308f.).

[91] Frag. in Jo. 51, (4:526).

[92] Peri Archon (hereafter PA) 2.4.4., (5:132). See also 4.2.1–2, (5:305–310). Obviously I can make no case based on this passage alone because of the problem of Rufinus's translation. I infer that this passage is substantially from Origen because of several other passages in his corpus to which I refer later.

[93] CC 4.72, (1:341); also Comm. on Mt. 15:11.

[94] Also CC 6.64, (2:134–51).

[95] PA 2.8.5, (5:162).

[96] Hom. in Gen. 3.2, (6:41).

[97] Frag. in 1 Sam. 15:9–11, (3:295–97). I believe Crouzel interprets this passage incorrectly (as well as Hom. on Jer. 20.2) when he states that God changes decisions in the light of Saul's changed attitude or that of the Ninevites. Origen clearly asserts God's foreknowledge (line 12–13, p. 296). Thus God need not and cannot change decisions. Henri Crouzel, Origene et la "conaissance mystique," 260.

Origen often emphasizes God's lack of emotion in his homilies. According to Pohlenz, *Homily 20 on Jeremiah* is one of the *Hauptstellen* expressing Origen's understanding of impassibility.[98] The key idea of this homily is that God's emotions are similar to ours, but only in name. Origen ascribes anger to God and to us, but in vastly different senses, which corresponds to the vast difference between the Logos itself and our words. This homily comes very close to a complete denial of the reality of God's anger and repentance by making their similarity to ours purely verbal. On the other hand, one can sense a contrary urgency to defend the truth of these texts in some way. The dilemma Origen faces as a philosophical theologian and homilist on Scripture is how to reconcile the philosophic doctrine of impassibility with the biblical teaching that God has feelings.

In another homily on Jeremiah the dilemma is equally sharp.[99] Repentance seems unworthy and obnoxious both to a wise person and to God. Origen simply cannot conceive of how one could simultaneously be repentant and wise. Contrary to 1 Kings 15:11 and Joel 2:12 God knows the future. So God is unable to choose badly and repent afterward. According to Num. 23:19 God does not act like man.[100] But in Prov. 3:12 and Deut. 1:31, God does. What is the solution in the case of divine repentance? For Philo, the Numbers passage is true, and those that contradict it are figurative. For Origen God does not act like humans in ruling nature because God makes no errors. But when divine providence immerses itself in human matters, it uses human senses, customs, and words to reflect our lowly condition.

God really does know whether Israel will repent or not. Therefore Scripture uses terms such as "repentance" to convert infants even as an adult might display an irate face to a child. God appears to be angry and repentant, but in fact is neither. Origen, like Philo, eliminates the literal meaning of passages about God's repentance and anger by arguing that the texts that

---

[98] *Vom Zorne Gottes,* 31.

[99] 18.1f., (4:150f.).

[100] In his homily on Num. 16:3 Origen interprets Num. 23:19 to refer to the fact that the divine "in nulla est passio." See Grant, *Early Doctrine,* 29.

refer to them are only pedagogical.[101] Thus he preserves divine
apatheia by doing away with God's emotions as portrayed by the
Bible, at least in the case of repentance.

The Impassibility of the Logos

Christian belief in the passion and death of the Incarnate Logos
presents yet another problem for Origen. Does the Logos actually suffer? Origen derives his answer from his understanding
of Jesus' soul. Origen gives the solution already in the *Peri
Archon* 2.6.2:

> The reality of each nature exists in one and the same person in
> such a way that nothing unworthy or unfitting may be thought to
> reside in that divine and ineffable existence, nor on the other hand
> may the events of his life be supposed to be the illusions caused by
> deceptive fantasies.

In the reply to Celsus's argument that God cannot suffer, be crucified, drink vinegar and gall, he says: "The person and the essence
of the divine being in Jesus is quite a different matter from that of
his human aspect."[102] Earlier in this work he writes: "Just as he
intentionally assumed a body whose nature was not at all different from human flesh, so he assumed with the body also its pains
and griefs. He was not lord of these so that he felt no pain."[103]

Origen strictly denies the suffering of the Logos: "The Word
remains Word in essence. He suffers nothing of the experience of
the body or the soul."[104] He repeatedly defends the reality of the
human soul of Jesus along with the divinity of the Logos. "For
after the Incarnation the soul and body of Jesus became very
closely united with the Logos of God."[105] Being quite aware of
the necessity to express the unity of soul and Logos in Christ,

---

[101] (3:160).

[102] CC 7.16, (2:167). The CC passages generally show that despite the problem of Rufinus's translation, the PA texts above represent Origen's thought.

[103] Ibid., 2.23, (1:151).

[104] Ibid., 4.15, (1:185).

[105] Ibid., 2.9, (1:136).

Origen argues the intimate relationship between the two: "We affirm that his mortal body and the human soul in him received the greatest elevation not only by communion but by union and intermingling, so that by sharing in his divinity he was transformed into God."[106] Origen's understanding of God as Father and Logos is clear: emotions, change, and suffering are simply impossible.

But as we have seen, Origen, like Clement before him, was not perfectly consistent; he says that God suffers a human passion when dealing with human things. This very inconsistency in the greatest of Eastern theologians is significant. Origen was more than a good Platonist. He was a Christian thinker deeply influenced by the Scriptures and by belief in the reality of the Incarnation. Even though his doctrine of the soul of Jesus allowed him to ascribe suffering to it rather than to the Logos, he was not completely satisfied with this solution.

AD THEOPOMPUM

The most interesting document in early Christianity to address the question of divine passibility is a treatise to Theopompus, extant only in Syriac, supposedly written by one of Origen's pupils, Gregory the Wonderworker, in the third century.[107] More than any

---

[106] Ibid., 3.41, (1:237). See also PA 2.6.3–5, (5:141–145). Origen held that Jesus' body was made incorruptible, giving it a divine quality. CC 3.41 (1:237–38). It was possible for it to be seen differently in accordance with the capacity of those who saw it. CC 6.77, (2:146). The Logos also changes in the perception of believers. See CC 2.64, (1:185–86); 4.18, (1:287–88).

[107] Although Gregory's authorship was defended some time ago by Ryssel, and recently by H. Crouzel, it has been seriously questioned by L. Abramowski. V. Ryssel, *Gregorius Thaumaturgus, sein Leben und sein Schriften* (Leipzig: L. Fernau, 1880); H. Crouzel, "La Passion De L'Impassible: Un essai apologétique et polémique du IIIe siècle" in *L'Homme Devant dieu: Mélanges offerts au Père Henri de Lubac*, vol. 1 (Paris: Aubier, 1963), 269–79; L. Abramowski, "Die Schrift Gregor des Lehrers 'Ad Theopompum' und Philoxenus von Mabbug" in *Zeitschrift für Kirchengeschichte* 89 (1978):277–90; see also A. Grillmeier, *Christ in the Christian Tradition* 1, 2nd ed. (Atlanta: John Knox, 1975), 233, n. 55. This text appears to be from Origen's time and is written by a Gregory, but its modalism makes it very unlikely that Thaumaturgus wrote it, given his Origenism. Since I have no knowledge of Syriac, I will depend on the Latin translation of J. B. Pitra in

other document, it reflects that side of Alexandrian theology that insists, despite the philosophical axiom of divine immutability and impassibility, that the God of Christian faith suffers.

The text begins with a certain Theopompus asking whether God is impassible. Gregory replies with another question: "How are we able to say that God is subject to passion, O Theopompus?" Theopompus states his dilemma: "If by nature God is impassible, it follows that he can never suffer even if he wanted to, since his nature would then be doing what was contrary to will."[108] Gregory argues that to place God under the restriction of necessity by opposing divine nature to divine will is blasphemous. "For if God cannot do what he wills, it certainly follows that great suffering befalls him, since the will of God would be subjected to his nature."[109] The omnipotent God can never be kept by his nature from doing what he wills, because God is superior to all things, able to do all things, and under no necessity. It is impious to take away the freedom of almighty God.

Theopompus asks whether an impassible nature is prevented from suffering human sufferings because it is happy and incorruptible. If divine nature does not prevent divine suffering, perhaps God's will for happiness does. "I ask therefore whether God is not prevented by himself from undergoing suffering, since he always is what he is, if we consider the impassibility of his nature."[110] Next Theopompus wonders whether the question is basically useless, as it is, if, as some say, the nature of God restricts his will. Perhaps the nature of God is more powerful than his will, and if so, the impassible God cannot suffer human sufferings even if God wills it.

Gregory replies that only in us can nature and will be contrary. God's will is always joined to God's essence, even if God submits to suffering when God is by nature impassible. Theopompus responds with yet another formulation of the same

---

Analecta Sacra Patrum Antenicaenorum collected by J. P. Martinus (Paris: Roger and Chernovicz, 1883), 4:363–76. It is not likely that this will weaken my analysis, since I deal only with the main ideas. Originally, the treatise was in Greek.

[108] Ibid., 2.364.
[109] Ibid.
[110] Ibid., 3.264.

question: "whether the nature of God is not prevented from suffering by itself, and whether an impassible substance does not prevent its own will from suffering."[111]

Gregory's definition of divine *passio* finally appears: "Suffering is true suffering, when God designs something useless and not advantageous to himself."[112] Because the divine purpose is the healing of the evil thoughts of men, God's freely chosen design to suffer is for our good. Suffering is not true suffering if it is useful and freely chosen, so divine impassibility is protected.

Thus, three elements distinguish ordinary suffering from God's. God's suffering is useful, salvific, and freely chosen. By implication the suffering of passible beings is useless, nonsalvific, and unwilled. A fourth element of difference is added to these, which further distinguishes divine suffering from the suffering of truly passible beings: God's suffering causes suffering to suffer because it conquers suffering itself. Indeed, Gregory claims that we would not even know that the impassible was impassible unless it suffered, and felt the power of suffering.

How does divine suffering conquer ours? God's conquest of death reveals divine impassibility. God enters the gates of death, but does not suffer death.[113] Unlike Greek heroes who sacrificed themselves, God, who does not need glory and is superior to sufferings, came to death willfully and without fear.[114] There is nothing shameful in a death that frees us from death. Divine suffering is proper and good, because it expels human sufferings, especially those that are corrupt and rooted in the human mind.[115] Not only is death destroyed, but sin as well. In the very last section, Gregory names the subject of this treatise. It is Jesus, king over all things, who, remaining what he was, destroyed sufferings by his own impassibility as the light destroys darkness.[116]

Is Gregory's argument sound? Has he demonstrated successfully that it is possible for an impassible divine being to

---

[111]Ibid., 5.366.
[112] Ibid., 6.366.
[113] Ibid., 8.369.
[114] Ibid., 12.372.
[115] Ibid., 13.272.
[116] Ibid., 17.276.

suffer? The answer is no. Human beings could also be impassible if they met Gregory's first three conditions. Are there not good historical examples of people who suffer usefully, salvifically, and freely? Are they not impassible in God's sense if we accept this argument? As to the fourth condition, that God's death destroyed death, was it God who died or the man Jesus?

The *Ad Theopompum* is a historically important, albeit unsuccessful, attempt to introduce suffering into God while preserving divine perfection. Belief in the Incarnation of the Son of God led the author to his discussion. Clement had already grasped in a fleeting way that the doctrine of divine impassibility did not completely satisfy Christian intuition. Origen discovered the connection between the revealed love of God the Son in the Incarnation, and the love of God the Father for the Son and for us. Certainly God is always the same and changes not. But God, Father and Son, truly feels the passion of love. The *Ad Theopompum* tries to show how God can truly suffer in Jesus and still be God. The author saw clearly that the philosophical understanding of divine impassibility could not do justice to the Christian claim regarding the Incarnation.

3

"I BELIEVE BECAUSE IT IS UNLIKELY"
The God of the Latins

TERTULLIAN

No one is more interesting to study, both as an individual and as a Christian thinker, than Tertullian (c. 160–240). He singlehandedly created the possibility of Christian theology among Latin writers, contributing many ideas but especially the terminology by which they could discuss theological questions. Although strongly influenced by Stoicism, Tertullian confronted the same problem as those who wrote in Greek. How was a Christian theologian to uphold the biblical portrait of a God who felt emotions, and who changed to provide for people? With such a portrait, how could Tertullian expect to gain philosophical respectability?

Some of the authors we will examine in this chapter were unwilling to allow philosophical axioms to overwhelm their sense, based on Christian scripture and tradition, that God has emotions and does change for the sake of providence. And for Tertullian, the Incarnation revealed a suffering God who changed, thus presenting the indispensable and inept dishonor of Christian faith.

In *On the Testimony of the Soul* Tertullian argues against Marcion (who lived in the middle of the second century) that the anger attributed to God in the Bible is a literal designation. Marcion had denied that emotions could belong to the God of Christianity. Because of the many passages in Hebrew Scripture which attribute unworthy characteristics such as emotions to the divine, in Marcion's "refined" view the Jewish God was a lesser deity than the God of Jesus and Paul.[1] Marcionites seemed to honor the God of Jesus by doing away with concern for knowing the world, and they did not ascribe anger to the divine. If God is angry, they said, God is passionate (*passionalis*), and that which is passionate is corruptible.

But for Tertullian the soul has a superior opinion. It knows and therefore fears God. "Whence, then, the soul's natural fear of God, if God cannot be angry? How is there any dread of Him whom nothing offends? What is feared but anger? Whence comes anger but from observing what is done?"[2] In Tertullian's view the soul needs to fear God and God's anger is necessary for that fear to be real.

Book 2, chapter 16, of Tertullian's work against Marcion contains Tertullian's most important discussion of divine passibility. He begins by stating the need for God's severity and for the emotions that accompany it, such as wrath, jealousy, and sternness. Emotions are as indispensable to severity as severity is to justice. Heretics think that "if God is angry and jealous and roused and grieved, He must therefore be corrupted and must therefore die."[3] They judge that the divine is like the human, hence that God must have the same passions that we do. Actually the reverse is true, Tertullian argues. The Marcionites should "discriminate between the natures (*substantias*) and assign to them their respective senses, which are as diverse as their natures require, although they seem to have a community of designation."[4] God has feelings in the supreme way that befits the divine nature.

---

[1] Marcion was opposed by Origen, and by all others who argued that the Jewish Scriptures were truly Christian. For Marcion, see E. C. Blackman, *Marcion and His Influence* (London: S.P.C.K., 1948); also the more recent book by Joseph R. Hoffman, *Marcion, On the Restitution of Christianity* (Chico, Calif.: Scholars Press, 1984).

[2] *De testimonio animae* 2 in *Corpus Scriptorum Ecclesiasticorum Latinorum* (hereafter CSEL) (Vienna, 1890), 20: 137.

[3] *Adversus Marcionem* 2.16.3 in *Corpus Christianorum. Series Latina* (hereafter CCL) (Turnholt: Brepols, 1954), 1: 493.

[4] 2.16.4, in ibid., p. 493.

Tertullian continues with the statement that we who are made in the divine image are thus emotionally similar to God:

> And this, therefore, is to be deemed the likeness of God in man, that the human soul have the same emotions and sensations as God, although they are not of the same kind, differing as they do both in their conditions (*status*) and their expressions (*exitus*) according to their nature.[5]

The distinction between God's emotions and ours arises from the fact that the divine essence is incorruptible and ours is not. For God to have emotions in a divine manner means possessing perfectly all emotions such as meekness, patience, mercy, and their parent, goodness. So also does God feel anger. Because of divine incorruptibility, God is affected by emotions only in a happy way. God will be angry but not irritated or tempted, moved but not subverted.[6]

Tertullian attempted to work out logical distinctions to express a rational understanding of divine passibility and mutability. He needed to show how God's emotions are different from ours, as well as similar, but this development remained incomplete. He concluded chapter 16 thus:

> He must use all (feelings) because of all (situations), as many senses as there are causes: anger because of the proud and whatever else hinders evil. So again, mercy because of the erring, and patience because of the impenitent, and preeminent resources because of the meritorious, and whatever is the work of good. All these feelings move Him in His own way, in which it is fitting that He should be moved (*pati*), and because of Him man is affected equally in his own way.[7]

We will see that Tertullian also says that God cannot become less or more, or be affected by time, but is eternally the same. Here, however, God can and must have negative emotions to be a judge, and further, all emotions in order to be God. God

---

[5] 2.16.6, in ibid., p. 493.
[6] 2.16.7, in ibid., p. 494.
[7] Ibid.

does not feel them as we do, but nevertheless experiences them somehow, and therefore changes emotionally in a manner that is appropriately divine. Although Tertullian does not describe specifically or define systematically how this can be, he understands God's feelings in comparison with our own, a comparison rooted in the relationship of humanity to God as God's image. God is truly related to the world and responsive to the peculiar situation of each person.

God's Goodness

Tertullian defended the goodness of the biblical Creator against Marcion's attack. For Marcion divine goodness absolutely distinguished the Christian from the Jewish God. Tertullian's description of God's goodness in relation to the world leads directly to another aspect of God's mutability. The *Adversus Marcionem* contains his most important discussions of this topic.[8]

Tertullian attempts to discover "certain rules for examining God's goodness." First, "All things in God should be natural and ingenerate (*ingenita*), in order that they may be eternal just like God's own state." If they naturally belong to God, the attributes will not be "accounted casual and extraneous, and thereby temporal and lacking eternity." God is eternal, so ought the divine attributes to be. But Marcion's God is not eternally good. He becomes so by saving mankind.

Second, "all properties of God ought to be as rational as they are natural." God's goodness must be reasonable. The goodness of Marcion's God, however, is irrational, because that God proceeded to save creatures not previously created or known.[9]

Thus third, as implied in 1.24, God's attributes must be perfect. Because it is temporal and irrational, and also because it does not save most people, the goodness of Marcion's God is imperfect. "So long, then, as you prefer your god to the Creator on the simple

---

[8] See esp. 1.22f. in ibid., p. 463f. Tertullian explains at great length why the goodness of the Creator is an eternal attribute (2.3, p. 477), and why only the Creator is good by nature (2.1.6, p. 476).

[9] 1.23, in ibid., p. 465–66.

ground of his goodness, and since he professes to have this attribute as solely and wholly his own, he ought not to have been lacking in it to anyone."[10] But even those whom Marcion's God saves have an imperfect goodness given to them, since only their souls are saved and not their bodies. Thus only part of the person is saved, and the more sinful of the two parts at that.

But divine goodness, as Marcion presents it, lacks something else as well: to be good in a divine way, God must be able to condemn. Goodness is incompatible with deity if God is only good. Marcion's God was imperturbable and listless,[11] could save only some, and could not condemn at all. This type of goodness is inappropriate to God, because it is unresponsive to the changing situations of human life. It is "neither ingenerate (*ingenitam*) nor rational nor perfect, but wrong (*improbem*) and unjust and unworthy of the very name of goodness."[12] A God who is only good in dealing with the human race is not good enough to be God. It is precisely this point that leads Tertullian to argue that God is mutable and passible, someone who does indeed have personal feelings:

> For it is, furthermore, at this point quite open to discussion whether God ought to be regarded as a being of simple goodness, to the exclusion of all those other attributes, sensations, and affections which the Marcionites indeed transfer from their god to the Creator, and which we acknowledge to be worthy characteristics of the Creator too.[13]

The sense of this passage is even stronger than the translation suggests: if any being is represented as divine without the attributes that express personal responsiveness to the world, it lacks a necessary aspect of deity and is therefore not truly divine.

Tertullian also argues that Marcion contradicts himself, because Marcion's God does truly have emotions. Marcion held that the good God, announced by Jesus, was a newcomer in the

---

[10] 1.24.3, in ibid., p. 467.
[11] 1.25.3, in ibid., p. 468.
[12] 1.25.1, in ibid., p. 468.
[13] 1.25.2, in ibid., p. 468.

affairs of the human race and therefore began to have a concern for our salvation. God began to feel. Second, the desire to be known and accepted now by us means that Marcion's God must have feelings of rivalry against the Creator, feelings that for Tertullian are in a certain sense even appropriate to the one God. When Marcion's God decided to entertain a concern for our salvation after such a long time of indifference, "did he not by this very fact become susceptible of the impulse of a new volition, so as palpably to be open to all other emotions? But what volition is unaccompanied by the spur of desire? Who wishes for what he desires not?"[14] Concern in Marcion's God gives rise to will, and will gives rise to desire to save humanity from the rule of the Creator God. Emotions necessarily arise that are appropriate to the adversary relationship created by this new concern for the human race: "anger, discord, hatred, disdain, indignation, spleen, loathing, displeasure."[15]

Some of these very same emotions belong to the Christian God in the role of judge, which God must be if God is good. God must experience emotions such as offense and anger, and must punish. God is not fully good without being the enemy of evil. Judgment without punishment is irrelevant to morality and religion; one must both love and fear the Lord.[16] Since Marcion's god cannot feel offense and anger, and cannot judge or punish, it cannot be God.

God's Justice

That humanity is good by creation is evident especially in the freedom of the will that we possess. Although God had previous knowledge of our fall and the power to prevent it, there was no divine interference with the liberty bestowed, a liberty that is part of human-created goodness. Since the human race fell, it became necessary for God to become a judge in order to remain good.

God's justice for Tertullian is in one sense an eternal attribute, and in another sense one that is temporal and responsive

---

[14] 1.25.4, in ibid., p. 469.
[15] 1.25.6, in ibid., p. 469.
[16] 2.13.1–5, in ibid., p. 489–91.

to the situation of sin. It is eternal, innate, and natural, as is goodness. Goodness created the world, justice arranged it. "Do not
suppose that His function as a judge must be defined as beginning when evil began, and so tarnish His justice with the cause
of evil."[17]

Nevertheless, divine justice takes on another function in the
world as the result of sin. "Up to the fall of man, therefore, from
the beginning God was simply good; after that He became a
judge both severe and, as the Marcionites will have it, cruel."[18]
When sin occurred, the goodness of God had an adversary and
divine justice acquired a new purpose: to direct God's goodness
against this adversary. The result was that the "divine goodness,
being interrupted in that free course whereby God was sponta-
neously good, is now dispensed according to the deserts of every
man; it is offered to the worthy, denied to the unworthy, taken
from the unthankful, and also avenged on all its enemies."[19] In
another place he writes that God is "good from His own (character), just in consequence of ours. For if man had never sinned, he
would simply and solely have known God in His superlative
goodness, from the attribute of His nature."[20] Justice is an extension of the divine goodness when it is a punishment for sin.

Tertullian meets a major objection to divine mutability.
Marcionites claim that God is inconstant if the divine judgments change over time.[21] Tertullian argues that the mark of a
good judge is to decide on the merits of the case at hand, in
terms of the present moment of a person's existence. God must
change judgments depending upon the goodness or evil of persons now. No one should think of God as completely rejecting
or choosing a person for life. God's capability to judge and decide rationally whether to accept or reject someone is an aspect
of divine providence.

Tertullian makes the same argument to affirm the invalidity
of Jewish religious institutions. "Let us not annul this power which

[17] 2.12.3, in ibid., p. 489.
[18] 2.11.1, in ibid., p. 488.
[19] 2.13.1, in ibid., p. 489.
[20] De resurrectione carnis 14, in CSEL 47: 42–43.
[21] Adv. Marc., 2.23.1–3, CCL 1: 500–501.

God has to reform the law's precepts answerably to the circumstances of the times, with a view to man's salvation."[22] Jewish religious institutions are no longer a valid response to God's will, according to Tertullian, because that will has changed.

In Book 2, chapter 24, of the work against Marcion, Tertullian discusses the same type of divine mutability with regard to 1 Sam. 15:11, where God "[regrets] . . . that I made Saul king." God's repentance in this case, as with the Ninevites, has a different meaning than it does for us. It is obvious from the Greek term for repentance that sin need not be involved for repentance to occur:

> For it will have no other meaning than a simple change of a prior purpose; and this is admissible without any blame even in a man, much more in God, whose every purpose is faultless. Now in Greek the word for repentance is formed not from the confession of a sin but from a change of mind, which in God we have shown to be regulated by the occurrence of varying circumstances.[23]

Thus for Tertullian there are good reasons for divine mutability and passibility. God has various emotions that are appropriate to goodness but also to justice. God changes to become the judge of human sinfulness; and God's will changes in accord with the changing circumstances of history. In each case the change is caused in God by changes in the temporal world. Tertullian's desire to include mutability in his description of God springs partially from what he conceives as logical necessity. But his major concern is to defend theologically the personal and active God of biblical faith in various relationships with the world. While Tertullian is not unique in having this concern, he expresses it more strongly than any other early Christian writer.

Although he is neither acute nor systematic enough in showing how God can be mutable and immutable simultaneously, Tertullian does see the religious and theological importance of God's mutability. In his polemical works he seems to become so involved in arguing against his opponents' theories that he

---

[22] *Adv. Judaeos* 2.10, CCL 2, p. 1343.
[23] *Adv. Marc.,* 2.24.8, CCL 1, p. 503.

does not recall previously developed immutability-mutability distinctions. On the whole, he does not distinguish carefully enough among the different types of God's immutability and God's mutability.

A number of authors have argued that Tertullian "capitulates" to Marcion in regard to divine mutability, an opinion based on a passage in the second book of the treatise against Marcion, and held by M. Pohlenz,[24] R. Cantalamessa,[25] and Jean-Claude Fredouille.[26] They appeal to this statement:

> Whatever attributes, therefore, you (Marcionites) require as worthy of God must be found in the Father, who is invisible and unapproachable and placid and (so to speak) the God of the philosophers, whereas those qualities which you censure as unworthy must be supposed to be in the Son.[27]

Tertullian is indeed attributing passibility to the Word. We shall see in *De carne Christi* how the Incarnation involves a certain type of divine mutability, but Tertullian probably does not have that in mind here. In this passage, he may vacillate but he does not capitulate. Fredouille himself admits this in effect by citing passages that occur later in the treatise in which Tertullian again states the legitimacy of divine anger.[28] The authors may see Tertullian's "capitulation" as a point in his favor, because they themselves see no alternative to absolute divine immutability and wish to see Tertullian as "coming around in the end."

God's Immutability

Like other early Christian theologians, Tertullian also holds that God is immutable. Various aspects of the divine character remain unchanged because God is eternal. In the treatise against

---

[24] *Vom Zorne Gottes*, 28, 42, 58.

[25] *La cristologia di Tertullian* Paradosis 18 (Fribourg: Edizioni Universitarie, 1962), 41.

[26] *Tertullien et la conversion de la culture antique* (Paris: Etudes Augustiniennes, 1972), 161–62.

[27] *Adv. Marc.* 2.27.6, CCL 1: 506–507.

[28] See 5.13.3, in ibid., p. 702; 5.19.8, p. 722.

Hermogenes, who held that matter was eternal, Tertullian argued as follows: Hermogenes holds that matter is eternal; but the attribute of eternity belongs to God alone, because it is essentially a divine property; if matter were eternal, it would be God. Tertullian continued:

> But God must be One, because that is God which is supreme (*summum*); but nothing can be supreme save that which is unique (*unicum*); but nothing can be unique if something can be put on a level with it; but matter will be put on a level with God, when it is authoritatively declared to be eternal.[29]

Further in the treatise, Tertullian argues that immutability is a property of eternity, and therefore of God, since mutability and temporality belong observably to matter. He says that "what is eternal does not change; obviously it would lose what it had been by becoming by the change what it was not, if it were not eternal."[30] The type of mutability which renders matter temporal is not simply change of any sort, but loss. Tertullian may have used the term *indemutabilis* of God in a precise sense to indicate that a particular type of immutability, that is, incapacity to become less, belongs to the eternal.[31] Eternity cannot belong to anything that changes for the worse.

> But then change (*demutatione*) for the worse has been admitted by matter, and if this is so, it has lost its condition (*status*) of eternity; it has, in short, died its natural death (*mortua est denique sua forma*). But eternity cannot be lost because, unless it cannot be lost, it is not eternity.

---

[29] *Adv. Hermog.*, 4.6, CCL 1: 400–401. See the translation of J. H. Waszink, *The Treatise Against Hermogenes* in *Ancient Christian Writers* (Westminster, Md.: Newman, 1956), vol. 24; also *Ad nationes* 2.3. Waszink schematizes Tertullian's argument in the following way on p. 110: 1.1 God = supreme; 2. supreme = unique; 3. Therefore God is unique (one). 2.1. unique = that to which nothing is equal; 2. God is unique; 3. Therefore nothing is equal to God. 3.1. Matter, if it is eternal, is equal to God; 2. Nothing is equal to God (= 1.3); 3. Therefore matter is not eternal. Tertullian gives this argument only in this treatise. See René Braun, *"Deus christianorum": Recherches sur le vocabulaire doctrinal de Tertullien* (Paris: Presses Universitaires de France, 1962), 42. For all of my references to this work, the pages are the same in the second edition (1977).

[30] 12.3, CCL 1, p. 407.

[31] See 2.2; 12.1; 12.3. Braun, *"Deus christianorum,"* 57.

Tertullian concludes: "Therefore it is incapable of change for the worse (*demutatione*), because if it is eternity it can be changed for the worse (*demutari*) in no way."[32] The use of the term *demutatio* and the context of the argument itself show that eternity cannot involve loss. Eternity and the incapacity to become less imply each other. Matter decays and is therefore not eternal, and because of his earlier argument (not eternal = not divine), it is not divine.

Another passage carries the same implication. God exists in "unimpaired integrity and ought not to be diminished (*minui*) or suspended (*intercipi*) or destroyed (*corrumpi*). Well, then, also His happiness (*felicitas*) would disappear if He ever suffered loss (*si quid patitur*)."[33]

If God as eternal cannot become less, neither can God become more. God is by definition the supreme, that *magnum summum*, existing in eternity. Against Marcion's second God of goodness, Tertullian must argue that God is one and that divine attributes cannot be shared. "God is not if God is not one." Tertullian then describes God as "the great supreme (*summum magnum*) existing in eternity, unborn (*innatum*), unmade (*infectum*), without beginning and without end."[34] Marcion must ascribe the property of eternity to his God because there can be no God without it. But eternity can only belong to the supreme being, who by definition of supreme is unique. And the unique is by definition one.

Since God is not temporal, neither is God mutable. "Eternity has no time. It is itself all time: it acts, it cannot then suffer." (*Quod facit, pati non potest*).[35] The type of immutability which eternity implies is the incapacity to be affected by time, which is a third type of immutability ascribed to God. God is incapable of

---

[32] 12.5, CCL 1, p. 407.

[33] *Ad nat.* 2.6.1, ibid., p. 50.

[34] *Adv. Marc.* 1.3.1–2, ibid., p. 443–44. God as *magnum summum* is an original description. See Braun, "*Deus christianorum*," 43. Also *Adv. Marc.* 1.7 and 9. In *De anima* 21.7 (CCL 2, p. 814) Tertullian gives nearly the same list of attributes to distinguish God from the soul. Here he also calls God *inconvertibilem*. This directly contradicts what he says in the *De carne Christi*, as we shall see. The term *inconvertibilem* is, however, missing from one manuscript of *De anima*. See CCL 2, 814, n. 46.

[35] *Adv. Marc.* 1.8.3, CCL 1, p. 449.

becoming less, because only matter can decay, cannot become more, because of being *summum magnum,* and cannot be affected by that which is temporal.

Thus Tertullian argues on the one hand that God has emotions and does change, but on the other that the divine is immutable and impassible. Is he confused? Can it be both ways? Norris is rightly puzzled by this inconsistency. The fact that Tertullian accepts the "Platonized doctrine of God and creation which he had inherited from his predecessors as normative Christian teaching," but is troubled by divine immutability needs an explanation. Norris suggests that Tertullian did not understand or come to terms with the "philosophical presuppositions of the theology he transmits."[36] It is also likely that Tertullian was trying to be more biblical and realized, unconsciously at least, that his philosophical presuppositions were inadequate for this task.

The historical consequence of Tertullian's inconsistency could have been important. If his thoughts on mutability and passibility had become more influential among Latin writers, they might have paved the way for a Western theology that took the divine emotions in Scripture more seriously than has been the case. Instead they were largely ignored, except, perhaps, by Lactantius.

Divine Mutability in the Incarnation

Tertullian wrote a treatise against the Marcionites specifically to take issue with their docetism, the *De carne Christi,* which was followed later by a work on the Incarnation directed against Praxeas (*Adversus Praxean*), a monarchian.[37] Problematically, in these two treatises he attempts to refute opposite theories. In *De carne Christi* Tertullian argues that the Word can in some reasonable sense become human and not merely take on the appearance of a man. He takes for granted the distinction between the Word and

---

[36] *God and World,* 112.
[37] See the discussion of the chronology of Tertullian's works in T. D. Barnes, *Tertullian: A Historical and Literary Study* (Oxford: Clarendon, 1971), 30–56.

the Father, and the divinity of the Word. The full humanity of Christ is the point of contention. The Platonic objection that because God cannot change God cannot become human lies behind the Marcionite argument against Jesus' full humanity.

Adversus Praxean takes the humanity of Christ for granted. The issue is whether there is a real distinction between the Father and Son. Therefore in this treatise Tertullian must argue that the Word is truly divine and yet truly distinct from the Father. The Logos must have all the divine attributes, including eternity and immutability, yet be distinct.

The *De carne* establishes the Word's mutability as a condition for the reality of the Incarnation. If Jesus is truly God, God's Word truly became flesh. Therefore Tertullian upholds the mutability of the Word against Marcion. Later, however, as a condition for divinity, he argues for the immutability of the Word against Praxeas. He does not develop a systematic viewpoint by which he can simultaneously defend the becoming of the Word and its immutability, thereby refuting both opponents.[38]

Marcionites say that the Incarnation is impossible: if God becomes what God previously was not, the divine identity disappears. Something without end is necessarily also inconvertible, since conversion into something else puts an end to what one originally was. There can be no conversion of something unending.[39] Tertullian admits that this is true for things in general, but nothing is the same for God.

> If, then, the things which differ from God and from which God differs lose what they were when they are converted, what will the difference of the divinity be from everything else except that

---

[38] *De carne* proposes mutability (*conversio*) as an explanation for the Incarnation, and *Adv. Praxean* denies it by denying the term *transfiguratio*. Although the two terms used for change do not have exactly the same sense, even in *Adv. Praxean* he states at least once (27.13) that the *conversio* of the Word in the Incarnation, for which he previously argued in *De carne,* is impossible. See Cantalamessa, *Cristologia,* 72f.

[39] *De carne* 3.4, CCL 2, p. 876.

the contrary obtains, i.e., that God can be converted into all things and continue as he is?[40]

Since God is not equal to creatures in any other respect, why would God be their equal in changeability (*in exitu conversionis*)?[41] Because of being divine, God can become anything, yet remain the same. The divine will need not obey the laws and dictates of creaturely possibility.[42]

The divine character is such that it can allow for change while retaining its identity, which is in this case an embodiment (*corporationem*) of the Word in Jesus.[43] It is correct to say that God was literally crucified, that God died and was buried, and that God rose from the dead. The fact that the docetic Marcionites deny this reality destroys the "indispensable dishonor of our faith."[44]

It must be noted that Tertullian never wrote the statement attributed to him so authoritatively by so many textbooks: "I believe because it is absurd." He was not a fideist. Here he is attempting to voice the paradox of Christian faith which sees the suffering God in the person of the crucified Jesus. He writes: "The Son of God is crucified. Because it is so shameful, it does not shame me. The Son of God dies. It is credible because it is so unlikely. The buried One rises. It is certain because it is impossible."[45] The cardinal point of Christian faith in the Incarnation is that it arises from the unlikely, shameful, and impossible fact that the Son of God died and rose from the dead. And for Tertullian this is fundamentally grounded in divine mutability.

---

[40] 3.5, in ibid., p. 876.

[41] 3.6, in ibid., p. 876–77.

[42] 3.1, in ibid., p. 875. "With God, however, nothing is impossible but what he does not will." Also in *Adv. Praxean* 10.9, ibid., 1170: "For with God, to be willing is to be able. All that He has willed, however, He has both been able to accomplish and has displayed His ability." Tertullian's understanding of God's will as active in history is unique in early Christian theology. See Norris, *God and World*, 118f. for this theme.

[43] *De carne* 4.1, CCL 2, p. 878.

[44] 5, in ibid., p. 880–83.

[45] 5.4, in ibid., p. 881.

Tertullian is the first Christian theologian to directly confront the problem of divine mutability which Christian belief in the Incarnation presents. Because of the obvious logical difficulty of his position in *De Carne* however, it is not surprising that he reverses it later. In *Adversus Praxean* he not only changes his terminology but even defends what he denied previously: the unchanging nature of the Word.

In *Adversus Praxean*, Tertullian again tries to explain the statement that the "Word became flesh."[46] Is the becoming a *transfiguratio* or a clothing (*indutus*) with flesh? Since God is unchangeable and incapable of form, being eternal, divine becoming can only mean the latter. Transfiguration involves the destruction of the previous existent: "For whatsoever is transfigured into some other thing ceases to be that which it had been and begins to be that which it previously was not. God, however, neither ceases to be what He was nor can He be any other thing than what He is."[47] Divine transfiguration into flesh is impossible.

If the Word becomes flesh by a change of substance, the resulting unity is a mixture, a *tertium quid,* neither God nor human. Tertullian uses the distinction of natures to interpret passages in the New Testament as applying to the human nature or to the divine, depending on the attribution. Neither the Father nor the divine Son is capable of suffering.[48] And even though the Spirit enables Jesus to suffer in the flesh and in us as well, the Spirit of God is also impassible.[49] Tertullian returns in the *Adversus Praxean* to the logic of the book against Hermogenes. He could not

---

[46] *Adv. Prax.* 27, in ibid., 1198–1200.

[47] 27.6–7, in ibid., p. 1198–99. Of all the authors I consulted, J. P. Mahé has the best view of the inconsistency between the two treatises. He explains it as a clarity of expression gained by the time the *Adv. Praxean* is written, and this represents an advance over the terminology of the *De carne*. See his introduction to *La chair du Christ* (Paris: Cerf, 1975), 150–155. *Conversio* in *De carne* means an absolutely unique change that preserves the unchanging essence of Christ. In *Adv. Praxean* Tertullian gives up the term *conversio* and explicitly rejects *transfiguratio* as an apt expression for the mutability that the Incarnation involves. He settles on the term *induere* (clothing).

[48] *Adv. Prax.* 29, in ibid., p. 1202–03.

[49] For Tertullian's use of *Spiritus Dei*, see Cantalamessa, *Cristologia*, 50–51. The term usually refers to the Son, emphasizing his consubstantiality. Here, however, it refers to the third person of the trinity. See p. 50 n. 1.

reconcile the mutability of the Son with the immutability of the divine essence.

Because the philosophical heritage was so negative about it, the incarnational mutability of God became difficult to conceptualize. For Plato, Aristotle, the Middle Platonists, and Plotinus, the truth of such a claim is unthinkable. In spite of this, Tertullian made real contributions to a theology of God which takes divine personhood seriously. God cannot change in the same manner in which we do, but change is essential to divine involvement in a changing world. God does not experience emotions as we do, but must have them to be involved in a world of persons precisely as a person. God's goodness demands mutability if God is perfectly good. A personal God is responsive to our needs, so much so, that the Word indeed became flesh and dwelled with us. This latter insight will begin to come into its own in the theology of the fourth century largely because of Athanasius.

Norris judges Tertullian correctly as a theologian committed to the Middle Platonism which he inherited from his predecessors, especially Justin and Irenaeus.[50] They insisted on divine immutability. Tertullian imbibed this philosophical tradition but also the Scriptures. Their difference on this point led him to diverge from the theology of his predecessors. God was, for him, necessarily mutable. Tertullian seems unaware of the difficulties inherent in joining the Platonic with the Scriptural portraits of God, and so never presents this conflict except perhaps rhetorically in his famous remark: "What does Athens have to do with Jerusalem?" This, along with his polemical intentions, prevented him from developing a more systematic view of God.

LACTANTIUS

Three Latin writers discuss divine immutability after Tertullian and before Hilary of Poitiers: Novatian, a Roman theologian; and

---

[50] Norris, *God and World*, 111–12.

two Africans, Arnobius of Sicca and his pupil Lactantius (c. 240–320). In reaction to his teacher's Epicurean theology, Lactantius wrote a treatise on divine anger in which he argued for the reality of God's emotions. The *De Ira Dei* (On God's Anger) is a presentation and defense of the doctrine of divine anger in the context of divine providence.[51]

Many persons, Lactantius says in chapter 1 of his treatise, hold that God is not angry, either because anger is in conflict with goodness or because God does not care about us at all. Because our innate ignorance regarding God has been taken away by revelation, we have better knowledge than those philosophers who hold one or the other opinion.[52] The first step in attaining true knowledge of God is the rejection of popular religion; the second (chap. 2) is for the mind to perceive that there is one supreme God, whose power and providence made the world and governs it. The third and final step is the acceptance of Jesus' teaching, which moves us to knowledge and worship of the true God.

Because he has discussed the first step in another book,[53] Lactantius begins with the second. There are those who accept the oneness of God but incorrectly understand the divine nature. They deny that God has any form or think that God is unmoved by affection, because every affection is a sign of weakness. Others take away anger from God but believe that God is kind. Lactantius lists all the possible solutions to the problem of God's emotions, and then proceeds to discuss each one (chap. 2). The possible solutions are: (1) God has anger but no kindness; (2) God has neither anger nor kindness (Epicurus); (3) God has kindness but no anger (Stoic); (4) God has both anger and kindness.

Lactantius excludes the first solution easily: to believe that God is only angry is unreasonable, incredible, and inconsistent with God's goodness. Against the second solution he says, if God is not moved (a quality pertinent to a living being), if God

---

[51] See E. F. Micka, *The Problem of Divine Anger in Arnobius and Lactantius* (Washington: Catholic University of America, 1943), 81–112.

[52] CSEL 27: 67–132.

[53] *Div. Inst.* 5–6, CSEL 19: 398–580.

does nothing unique and worthy as governor of the world, God simply does not exist. What happiness could be in God if God were inactive, at rest and immovable, deaf to those who pray to Him, and blind to worshipers? Providence is worthy of God. The Epicurean view is excluded on the grounds that if God feels nothing whatsoever, there is no concern for the world and no divine providence. If divine concern and providence disappear, so does divine reflection and perception, and therefore divine existence (chap. 4).

He rejects the third solution as well. If one emotion is felt by God, so must its opposite, since opposite external circumstances call for opposite emotions (chap. 5). To be consistent, God must feel hatred for the wicked people just as much as love for the good, because loving good people is connected to hatred of the wicked, and hating the wicked to loving the good. To love, one must also hate, since some ought to be loved and some ought to be hated. Lactantius does not believe that a Christian should repress negative feelings; they are appropriate to some life situations.[54] Besides, the emotional life has a unity of its own, an integral movement in us and in God which cannot be set aside (chap. 4).

God experiences anger as well as kindness. All of piety and religion depends upon this understanding (chap. 6). Lactantius proceeds to explain why religion is necessary for us (chaps. 7–8). Religion is necessary to maintain human wisdom which separates us from animals and for justice, by which the public life may be maintained. Removing God's kindness or anger or both, removes religion. Removing religion, in turn, removes that which is uniquely human and the fear of the Lord's punishment which is necessary for the social order (chap. 12).

In chapter 15 Lactantius makes a necessary distinction about God's emotions: God feels some and not others. God cannot have fear, for God has neither desire nor injury nor pain nor death, which are the causes of fear. God can do whatever God wishes, and therefore envies no one (chap. 13). God has no sexual passion,

---

[54] 6.15, in ibid., p. 536–39.

no need of a successor or consort, no avarice nor grief (chap. 16). But favor, anger, and pity have their occasion in God as well as does patience (chap. 20). Each of God's emotions is a fitting providential response to some historical circumstance (chap. 16).

Lactantius's theology of God rests on this crucial point. God has whatever emotions God needs to have to govern. God does not, however, experience feelings that conflict with divine perfection. Both Novatian and Arnobius argued against real divine feelings on the ground that that which feels is corruptible. Tertullian distinguished between emotions and corruptibility, holding that they do not necessarily imply each other. Lactantius simply turns around the corruptibility argument formulated by Arnobius. Corruptibility belongs only to the unfeeling being. To be absolutely at rest is to be dead. God is eternally alive and never at rest in the divine governance. Therefore God is not corrupted by emotions, but God is a living God precisely because of them (chap. 17).

Lactantius describes the divine anger in a way that makes it worthy of God. It is reasonable and wise and justifiable if its motive is the correction of evil, as it is for God, and not vengeance. It belongs to us and to God alike, but God always feels it at the right time and place (chaps. 18 and 21). Finally, divine anger is necessary for the preservation of God's authority (chap. 23). Lactantius's treatise on divine anger shows how important it was for him to maintain divine personality. Without it and the emotions that accompany it, the Christian doctrine of providence is lost. The Christian view of providence and divine personhood cannot be rendered in a consistent and meaningful religious way if one adheres strictly to the Middle Platonist or Epicurean conception of God's transcendent immutability.

Nevertheless, Lactantius like Tertullian also describes God in the familiar manner of patristic theology. The divine is "impassible, immutable, incorrupt, blessed, and eternal."[55] God is one and perfect,[56] "incomprehensible and unspeakable, and fully

---

[55] 2.8, in ibid., p. 137: "inpassibilis inmutabilis incorruptus beatus aeternus."
[56] 1.3, in ibid., p. 7f.

known only to Himself."[57] The doctrine of God is summarized in the *Epitome of the Divine Institutes:*

> There is, then, one God, perfect, eternal, incorruptible, incapable of suffering, subject to no circumstance or power, Himself possessing all things, ruling all things, whom the human mind can neither estimate in thought nor mortal tongue describe in speech.[58]

NOVATIAN

Novatian's major dogmatic treatise, *De trinitate,* "was probably written well before 250 and is the first great Latin contribution to theology to appear in Rome."[59] A portion of this work, chapters 4–7, discusses divine immutability and God's wrath. Somewhat later Arnobius would write an apology for Christianity (*Adversus nationes*) in which the doctrine of God's immutability became the major theological idea. Lactantius apparently disagreed strongly enough with his teacher Arnobius that he wrote a treatise of his own defending the reality of God's wrath, as we have seen.

Novatian's work on the Trinity discusses the nature and attributes of God at some length.[60] The Christian doctrines of God's fatherhood, omnipotence, and creation are required by the rule of faith (*regula fidei*).[61] God has no beginning and no end. As a result God is always infinite (*semper immensus*) and there is nothing greater, and is always eternal because there is nothing older. That which is without origin is preceded by none, because it is not temporal.[62]

---

[57] 1.8, in ibid., p. 29.

[58] 3, in ibid., p. 678.

[59] Joannes Quasten, *Patrology* (Westminster, Md.: Newman Press, 1950), 2: 217. For the work itself see J. P. Migne, *Patrologiae Cursus Completus: Series Latina* (Paris: n.p., 1865), 3: c. 913–82.

[60] Chap. 2–8 in ibid., c. 915–27.

[61] This may have been the original title of the work. See R. DeSimone, *The Treatise of Novatian the Roman Presbyter on the Trinity: A Study of the Text and the Doctrine* (Rome: Institutum Patristicum Augustinianum, 1970). See also his translation, *The Trinity* (Washington: Catholic University of America, 1974) 67; p. 23 n. 1 discusses the title.

[62] 2, PL 3, c. 916.

God does not change or become transformed into other forms, lest by change the divine appear to be mortal. Novatian's argument against divine mutability recalls Tertullian. But for Tertullian change does not necessarily imply mortality; for Novatian it does. "For change (*immutatio*) implied in turning from one thing to another (*conversionis*) is comprehended as a portion (*portio*) of a certain death."[63]

In the same passage Novatian connects immutability to divine perfection. "Thus there is never in Him any accession (*adjectio*) or increase (*accedit*) of any part or honor, lest anything should appear to have ever been wanting to His perfection." If anything increases in God, it implies that God had a beginning, and if God loses anything, it indicates possible death and perishing. But that which constitutes divinity must necessarily always exist and have no beginning and no end. God must always be the same to be God, and is the same because of having no beginning. Novatian gives Tertullian's argument from *Hermogenes* 4.3, which deduces God's oneness from divine eternity:

> And thus (because of no beginning) He is declared to be one, having no equal. For whatever can be God must as God be of necessity the highest. But whatever is the highest must certainly be the highest in such a sense as to be without any equal. And thus that must needs be alone and one on which nothing can be conferred, having no peer.[64]

The argument surprisingly concludes that God is infinite rather than immutable or perfect. Novatian apparently confuses infinity with immutability or perfection, since the attributes all imply no beginning or end: "there cannot be two infinites, as the very nature of things dictates. And that is infinite which neither has any sort of beginning nor end."[65]

Despite his defense of divine immutability, Novatian also defends the divine wrath, indignation, and even hatred in a manner reminiscent of, if not dependent upon, Tertullian. We are not to understand these emotions "in the sense in which they are human

---

[63] 4, in ibid., c. 919.
[64] 4, in ibid., c. 920.
[65] Ibid.

vices," since God is incorruptible. "For such passions as these will rightly be said to be in men and will not rightly be judged to be in God."[66] God has these passions but is not corrupted by them because God does not have them properly.

The passible nature of humanity as opposed to the impassible nature of God allows us to distinguish between the wrath of the two. These passions are rightly felt by an embodied individual. Since God is not embodied, God does not have them properly. In the following chapter, Novatian argues against anthropomorphic conceptions of the deity, despite the biblical passages to the contrary.

In this treatise Novatian wants to argue for divine immutability as well as for divine wrath but is unable to reconcile these two doctrines because he lacks Tertullian's sense of the analogical character of language about God. Ultimately he rests his case on God's incomprehensibility. Chapter 7 states this quite forcefully: God is something like us in divine feelings of wrath, indignation, and hatred, but we simply do not know how God is like us, because the divine is incomprehensible. Neither can we speak properly of God. "We can in some degree be conscious of Him in silence, but we cannot in discourse unfold Him as He is."[67] God cannot be literally construed as Love or Light or Spirit or Fire, because of being greater than any merely human description. We can speak of God as having human passions, but these have no objective application to God's incomprehensible being.

ARNOBIUS

In his *Against the Nations*, written around 296, Arnobius completely rejected all theological attempts to justify God's emotions. His major concern was to differentiate the Christian God from the popular deities of his time, and his understanding of God shows the influence of Epicurus.[68] The Epicurean idea of God as aloof

---

[66] 5, in ibid., c. 921.
[67] 2, in ibid., c. 916.
[68] George E. McCraken, *Arnobius of Sicca: The Case against the Pagans* in *Ancient Christian Writers* (Westminster, Md.: Newman, 1949) 7–8, p. 29–30.

from the concerns of the world "runs through all of *Adversus nationes*, and is really its central thought, the fountainhead of all its teaching."[69]

The *Against the Nations* strongly condemns the passionate gods and goddesses of paganism. They are much too involved in the affairs of the world, and the actions and passions that the myths attribute to them are unworthy of the divine. When the enemies of Christianity, for instance, say that their gods are angry at Christians, do they not see that they are attributing base feelings to them? "For to be angry, what else is it than to be insane, to rave, to be urged to the lust of vengeance?"[70]

True gods have no anger or grudges. It is "childish, weak, petty, and unbecoming" for pagan gods to "be busied with the coarser matter of earth,"[71] and it is a sacrilege to believe that God feels despised if worship is not given. The Christian God does not need prayers. These only benefit us by bringing us closer to God.[72]

Arnobius often draws the same connection between feelings and corruptibility which we have noted previously. The gods should not have emotions since those who are "touched by passion live a life of suffering and are weakened by grief." They are therefore "bound by the laws of mortality."[73] Whatever is liable to suffering is corruptible "by that very capacity of suffering,[74] he says, referring to the soul. And "whatever is upheld by causes and things external to itself must be mortal and on the way to destruction, when anything on which it lives begins to be wanting."[75] For a summary statement, we return to the beginning of the work:

> For wherever, as the philosophers hold, there is agitation, there of necessity passion must exist. Where passion is situated, it is reasonable that mental excitement (*perturbatio*) follows. Where there is mental excitement, there grief and sorrow exist. Where grief and

---

[69] Quasten, *Patrology* 2:388.
[70] 1.17, CSEL 4:13.
[71] 1.23, ibid., 5.
[72] 1.27, ibid., 17–18.
[73] 6.2, ibid., 214–15.
[74] 2.26, ibid., 69–70.
[75] 7.3, ibid., 239.

sorrow exist, there is already room for weakening (*imminutione*) and decay (*corruptioni*).[76]

He repeats this argument in almost the same form near the end of the work: feeling is being moved by another. Whatever is moved by another is capable of suffering and frailty and must therefore be corruptible. Anger is a feeling and thus it renders the angered being corruptible. "Therefore that should be called mortal which has been made subject to the emotions of anger."[77] But God is immortal; therefore God cannot be angry.

CONCLUSION

Despite his incapacity to construct a consistent doctrine of God, Tertullian's descriptions of divine emotions and mutability suggest interesting theological possibilities. For him God had to change to adopt a new attitude to a new situation, that is, to human sinfulness, and had to feel appropriate emotions in order to judge as well as to love people properly. Also, as historical circumstances changed, so necessarily did God's will for us.

Lactantius squarely faces the question of divine emotions and mutability. He argues that God must relate to the world in a providential manner, and that this relation must include emotions. Both he and Tertullian saw, however, that God must have emotions only in some distinctively divine manner, either by feeling only the most appropriate emotions or by having all emotions perfectly.

Novatian argued for God's emotions, especially for divine wrath, but did less with his argument than Tertullian because he eventually appeals to God's incomprehensibility. Out of concern to distinguish the Christian God from the many deities of Greece and Rome, Arnobius denies entirely the possibility of divine emotions and mutability. He appeals, one might suggest, to Epicurus.

---

[76] 1.18, ibid., 13–14.
[77] 7.5, ibid., 241.

We will see later that Augustine rejects the possibility of emotion and mutability applying literally to God. Augustine consistently asserts divine immutability and impassibility, thereby intensifying if not creating several classical theological problems such as creation in time by an unchanging being, predestination, and divine foreknowledge of the future. If we look to Augustine's Christology, however, something new appears. The next chapter will show how Athanasius partially reformulated the Christian understanding of God in opposition to the Christology of Arius, yet affirmed, as did his opponent, the divine descent. Ultimately Augustine inherited Athanasius's reformulated notion, and so was strongly affected by descent imagery. Although he did not absorb it fully, the imagery dramatically affected Augustine's understanding of God's immutability and impassibility.

4

THE SUFFERING GOD
Arians and the Orthodox

The full debate about the distinctive nature of the Christian God erupted in the Trinitarian and christological controversies of the fourth and fifth centuries. Even before the Council of Nicea (325) Alexandrian theologians tended generally to think in terms of a Logos-sarx or Word-flesh scheme that emphasized the divinity sometimes at the expense of the human Jesus. The Gospel of John was their favorite text, especially the "Word became flesh" of 1:14. Athanasius (c. 295–373) had so absorbed the Alexandrian model that some scholars criticize his neglect of the soul of Jesus even today.[1]

Both the followers of Arius (c. 260–336) and Apollinaris (c. 310–390) shared this aspect of Athanasius's Christology, believing that it kept them from accepting the conclusion that Jesus was a mere man. Yet they drew opposite conclusions. While Arius denied the full divinity of the Word and Apollinaris the

---

[1] The question of Jesus' human soul in Athanasius need not be addressed here. The explanation that seems best to me is that of C. Stead, "The Scriptures and the Soul of Christ in Athanasius," *Vigiliae Christianae* 36, no.3 (September, 1982) 233: "Athanasius's whole understanding of the humanity assumed by the Logos implies the presence of a soul."

full humanity of Jesus, Athanasius held to the single divine personhood of Jesus, and to his full humanity.

In spite of legitimate contemporary reaction to and criticism
of the Word-flesh Christologies of the Alexandrians, "it must
be admitted that, viewed within its soteriological context, their
position is consistent and religiously compelling. The Logos
himself took over our flesh, shared our experience, and overcame our weaknesses and sin by his divine power."[2]

Although fourth-century Alexandrian thought did not reject
the Greek philosophical heritage, out of Arianism and anti-Arian
responses a "paradox" emerges because of a growing awareness of
a conflicting truth: in spite of the divine attributes of perfect
changelessness and the incapacity to suffer, God's divine Word
did somehow suffer with us and for us. The rise of Arianism sig-
nals the end of the period in which Christian thinkers can construct an understanding of God solely by recourse to ancient
Greek philosophical resources. Athanasius understood this, according to Kannengiesser, and argued that the Arians were:

> mistaken in their concept of theology because they believe they are
> able to form a Christian idea of God by first developing in isolation
> the theory of the divinity of the Father and the Son, without taking
> into consideration right from the start the mystery of the incarna-
> tion of the Son.[3]

Kannengiesser says further, this "Athanasius Christocentrism" is
an "astonishing innovation" in an Alexandrian theology that was
so thoroughly dominated by Origen. Athanasius is the first
Christian author to publish a treatise *On the Incarnation of the
Word* because he saw that "that which is first in the exposition of
the Christian faith is not God as such, nor the universe in its
divine origin, but the historical event of salvation accomplished
in Christ."[4]

---

[2] F. M. Young, "Reconsideration of Alexandrian Christology," *Journal of Ec-
clesiastical History* 22 (1971): 105.

[3] Charles Kannengiesser, "Athanasius and Traditional Christology," *Theological Studies* 34 (1973): 112.

[4] Ibid.

We will see later that a more recent view of the matter is possible. It is one that gives some credit to the Arians for this "astonishing innovation," arguing that it was indeed they who saw the need for a Christian understanding of incarnation which allowed for the reality of divine suffering.[5]

The Christology of the school of Antioch emphasized the full and real humanity of Jesus. It depended upon the more dynamic and religious Alexandrian thinking and became its rational corrective. The Christology of two complete natures in Jesus—one human, one divine—developed at the council of Chalcedon in 451 was an attempt to relegitimate the Alexandrian view as reflected at Nicea (325) and Ephesus (431), and to allow for its critique as well, lest the God who became human in Jesus did not really come at all (Arius), or did not become fully human (Apollinaris).

THE CRUCIFIED GOD OF THE ARIANS

An interesting theological interpretation of Arianism is one of the most recent, that of R. P. C. Hanson, who writes that "at the heart of the Arian Gospel was a God who suffered." Arians wanted "to be faithful to the Biblical witness to a God who suffers."[6] Hanson explains the lowering of the Word to a status

---

[5] This was developed recently by the late R. P. C. Hanson in "The Arian Doctrine of the Incarnation," in Robert C. Gregg, ed., *Arianism: Historical and Theological Reassessments* (Philadelphia: The Philadelphia Patristic Foundation, 1985), 181–211; *The Search for the Christian Doctrine of God: The Arian Controversy 318–381* (Edinburgh: T. & T. Clark, 1988).

[6] *The Search,* p. 121. For Arius and Arianism in general see especially Christopher Stead, "The Freedom of the Will and the Arian Controversy," in *Platonismus und Christentum, Festschrift für Heinrich Dörrie,* ed. H.-D. Blume and F. Mann, *Jahrbuch für Antike und Christentum Ergänzungsband* 10 (Münster - W: Aschendorff, 1983), 245–57; Maurice Wiles, "In Defence of Arius," *Journal of Theological Studies* 13 (1962): 339–47; Robert C. Gregg and Dennis E. Groh, *Early Arianism: A View of Salvation* (Philadelphia: Fortress, 1981), 68, 161; "The Centrality of Soteriology in Early Arianism," *Anglican Theological Review* 59 (1977): 260–78; J. N. D. Kelly, *Early Christian Doctrines,* rev. ed. (New York: Harper, 1978); A. Grillmeier, *Christ in the Christian Tradition,* 2nd ed., (Atlanta: John Knox, 1975) 1: 219–45. For bibliographical material from 1960 on for this entire chapter, see the end of Frances Young, *From Nicea to Chalcedon* (Philadelphia: Fortress, 1983). The most recent attempt to reconstruct the sources is Rowan Williams, *Arius: Heresy and*

that was less than divine as a logical implication of Arian belief
in the suffering of the Word, as follows:

> The Arians saw that the New Testament demanded a suffering
> God, as their opponents failed to see. They were convinced that
> only a God whose divinity was somehow reduced must suffer.
> Hence the radical Arian doctrine of Christ, but hence also the
> Arian readiness to speak of God as suffering.[7]

So it is that Arian thought made a contribution to the Christian
theology of incarnation. It "achieved an important insight into the
witness of the New Testament denied to the pro-Nicenes of the
fourth century, who unanimously shied away from and endeav-
ored to explain away the scandal of the Cross."[8]

Hanson bases his argument on the fact that Arians generally
had no doctrine of the human soul of Jesus, and stated strongly
that the Word suffered. This is especially true in the *Homilies on
the Psalms* of Asterius the Sophist (died c. 341).[9] Of this work
Hanson writes, "Everything that he says . . . suggests that he
believes in a God who can suffer."[10]

In one such statement regarding the crucifixion, Asterius
says, "Do not say a mere man was killed, but God in flesh making
the suffering and the death of the flesh his own."[11] He speaks of
God as crucified, *theon estaurōsan,*[12] and of the Incarnation as the
place where God revealed condescension, love, and providence.[13]

Hanson also appeals to the two Arian homilies in Greek
given on the octave of Easter preserved under the name of John

---

Tradition (London: Darton, Longman and Todd, 1987), especially Part 1. See his
bibliography as well as Hanson's.

[7] Hanson, *The Search,* 41.

[8] Ibid., 122.

[9] Marcel Richard, *Asterii Sophistae Commentariorum In Psalmos Quae Super-
sunt Accedunt Aliquot Homiliae Anonymae* (Oslo: A. W. Brogger, 1956). Useful for
a study of this work is Eiliv Skard, *Index Asterianus* (Oslo: Universitetsforlaget,
1962).

[10] Hanson, *The Search,* 38.

[11] *Hom.* 22.2–3 in *Asterii Sophistae,* p. 173. Also *Hom.* 2.6, p. 6.

[12] *Hom.* 2.3; *Hom.* 2.6; in ibid., 5, 6.

[13] *Hom.* 25.25, in ibid., p. 198: *synkatabasin, philanthrōpian, epopteian.* See also
Hom. 4.13, p. 51; frag. on p. 255, line 8. Other texts cited in Hanson, *The Search,*
38–41.

Chrysostom (c. 354–407).[14] The term *enanthrōpēsas* (translated "incarnation," but literally "in-humanization") is used twice for the divine descent,[15] and at one point the homilist states boldly: "God was not unwilling to suffer on the cross."[16] The prayer of a just one truly inclines the divinity toward pity,[17] and prayer brings the divine judge to compassion.[18] The Arian homilist is not afraid to call the Word *ho monogenēs theos,* the only begotten God.[19]

It is interesting that in a passage of the first homily, Liebaert finds a pro-Nicene interpolation in the statement that God, not a divine Word that was less in divinity, suffered:

> He assumed that which is of humanity for humanity. . . . He did not transform the better into worse; he did not change more into less; the putting on of flesh does not change the nature of divinity; the assumption of the flesh does not diminish the hypostasis of the only begotten.[20]

This passage is followed by another interesting sentence: "He endured fatigue, the untiring artisan of creation."[21] *Homily* 1.24 also attributes suffering to a God who is fully God. Liebaert attributes this to homiletic excess.[22] Simply because these are Arian homilies, however, need not rule out the authenticity of the statements above. The homilies may be authentically Arian, which would indicate the kind of ambiguity the tradition has always felt among both heterodox and orthodox about the issue of divine suffering, and perhaps about the full divinity of the Word, at least on the Arian side.

---

[14] J. Liebaert, ed., *Deux Homelies Anomeenes pour l'Octave de Paques* (Paris: Les Editions Du Cerf, 1969) Sources Chretiennes, v. 146.
[15] *Hom.* 1.15.213, in Liebaert, *Deux Homelies,* p. 76. Also in 2.13.169, p. 108. See also *Hom.* 15.17, in Richard, *Asterii Sophistae,* p. 115.
[16] *Hom.* 1.24.344–45 in Liebaert, *Deux Homelies,* p. 88.
[17] *Hom.* 2.1.7–8, in ibid., p. 94.
[18] *sympatheian. Hom.* 2.2.29, in ibid., p. 96.
[19] *Hom.* 2.1.25–26, in ibid., p. 96.
[20] *Hom.* 1.2.31–33, in ibid., p. 58.
[21] *Hom.* 1.3.37, in ibid., p. 58.
[22] *Hom.* 1.24.344–45, in ibid., p. 88. See 36–37 for Liebaert's comments.

One of the most remarkable passages in this Arian literature asserting divine suffering comes from the *Unfinished Work on Matthew*, which was also ascribed to John Chrysostom, although it was probably written in Latin by an Arian of the fifth century.[23]

> Where is the scandal of the cross of Christ? What would scandalize us if a mere man died? Unbelievers perish because they know that if God came, God would die, and if God died, God could not be God. Believers are saved because they know that Christ did not die because of the weakness of human nature, but drew death to himself by means of divine power. Thus God was not absorbed by death but absorbed it. Therefore we do not believe that Christ died on the cross, but that death died in Christ.[24]

This same homilist can also say later that the Word of God "put human salvation above his own impassibility."[25]

Rowan Williams makes an interesting comment about Hanson's understanding of this insight of Arianism, that it "is held at the high price of postulating 'two unequal gods'; only Nicaea can actually do justice to a doctrine that the Nicene Fathers would have rejected—the self-sacrificing vulnerability of God." The fact that Arians had the right idea about divine suffering but that it led them to the wrong idea of God "puts the unavoidable question of what the respective schemes in the long term make possible for theology." The answer for Hanson, in Williams's view, is perhaps an "odd conclusion that the Nicene fathers achieved not only more than they knew but a good deal more than they wanted."[26]

---

[23] *Opus Imperfectum In Matthaeum,* in PG 56, 612f.

[24] My translation. 30.39, c. 788. Notice how far removed this is from the idea based on the two complete natures of Christ, that only the human nature of Christ died. Here as I have argued throughout this book, it seems evident that something crucial is at stake, which ancient philosophy and modern variations thereof simply cannot accept.

[25] "Sui ipsius impassibilitati praeposuit salutem humanam." 51.47, c. 928. For Hanson's complete case about Arian insistence on a suffering God based on these and several other sources, see especially *The Search,* p. 109–28.

[26] *Arius: Heresy,* 22.

ATHANASIUS

For Athanasius the Word shares the divine attributes of the Father, being *atreptos* and *analloiōtos* by essence. Thus the defense of the divinity of the Word consists in the transference of divine attributes to the Word[27] with one important difference: the Word became flesh, and now flesh must be attributed to God.

> The incorporeal Word made his own the properties of the body, as being his own body. . . . For what the human body of the Word suffered, this the Word, dwelling in the body, took upon (*anepheren*) himself, in order that we might be enabled to be partakers of the Godhead of the Word.[28]

God becomes human so that humans may partake of God, and because of the Incarnation the impassibility and immutability of the Logos become important for salvation. Unless the divine Word remains the same, we cannot become like it ourselves. The Logos carried my *pathē*, although being *apathēs*, "and so I became free" from passion, Athanasius says.[29] The problematic nature of this claim, however, did not escape him: "And truly it is paradoxical that he it was who suffered and yet suffered not. Suffered, because his own body suffered, and he was in it, which thus suffered; suffered not, because the Word, being by nature God, is *apathēs*." Because the impassible Word was in the passible body of Jesus, it destroyed the body's weaknesses in order to do away with them in us and to "invest us with what was his," that is, immortality.[30]

---

[27] *Discourse* 1, 49B; 57A; 84C; 93B; 112C; *Disc.* 2, 160B; 168A; 220A in PG 26. For several christological references to *atreptos* and *analloiōtos* in Athanasius see G. Muller, ed., *Lexicon Athanasianum, digessit et illustravit* (Berlin: W. de Gruyter, 1952).

[28] *Letter 59 to Epictetus* 6, c. 1060C in PG 29.

[29] *Disc.* 3, 397A; 437B; 440A in PG 26. For *apatheia* as a religious goal in the fourth century, see the Prologue to Palladius's *Lausiac History*, vol. 34 of *Ancient Christian Writers*.

[30] *Letter 59 to Epictetus* 6, c. 1060 in PG 29.

When the flesh of Jesus suffered, the Logos was not external to it. Therefore, pathos is said to be his.[31] The suffering of his body, however, did not touch him in his divinity.[32] The Son of God remained *atreptos* and *analloiōtos* in the human economy and in the enfleshed presence that he had.[33] The assumption of the flesh (*proslēpsis tēs sarkos*) did not make a servant of the Word who was by nature Lord.[34] "He is impassible and incorruptible and the very Word and God, but he cared for and saved suffering humanity, for whom he endured these things, by his impassibility."[35]

Athanasius's vision of the Incarnation of the Word is religiously compelling, but not logically so. The Antiochene critique emphasizes the presence of the human soul of Jesus, and "solves" the problem of the human suffering of the Word by denying it. All the suffering of Jesus takes place in his human body and soul. Yet this answer creates the new problem of unity of person. Either the Logos suffers and changes, or it does not. If it does, both Arius and Athanasius believe, it is not divine. If it does not, Athanasius implies, we are not saved. Can the Impassible suffer? Yes, but only if, as the *Ad Theopompum* argued, there is more than one meaning for one or the other term. Divine suffering must be different from our imperfect sufferings, or we are involved either in a denial of divinity or in a contradiction.

Although Athanasius never resolves this question, he says several times that the Logos exhibited *synkatabasis* or condescension in the Incarnation, thereby changing in some way. In three places in the *De Incarnatione* and in six texts of the *Discourses*, the term appears either in reference to creation or Incarnation.[36] In creation God's wisdom imposes its form on the world[37] which is a

---

[31] *dia toute gar autou legetai kai to pathos.*
[32] *Disc.* 3, 389C in PG 26.
[33] *Disc.* 2, 160B in ibid.
[34] Ibid., 176C.
[35] *De Incarnatione* 54.15.
[36] See C. Kannengiesser's Introduction to *De Incarnatione* in *Sources Chretiennes* vol. 199, p. 129. He cites four instances in the *Discourses* rather than six. I discovered another in *Disc.* 2, 277C in PG 26 and am also counting a non-Athanasian text from *Disc.* 4, 516C in ibid.
[37] *Disc.* 2, 312B and 317B in ibid.

form of divine condescension. It is an indirect divine lowering
mediated through wisdom. In the Incarnation, however, it is different. After creation the Logos descended and assimilated with
that more complete work.[38] The Logos is first-born because of
lowering himself down to be with creatures, resulting in God
becoming the brother of all.[39] Athanasius also gives the motive for
the divine condescension in the Incarnation. The Word conde-
scended because of our weakness,[40] and out of love,[41] pity, and
mercy.[42] The Incarnation is divine and loving condescension.[43]

This theme of divine lowering, already portrayed by Origen,
Clement, and *Ad Theopompum*, is an intuitive grasp of the Christian truth that conflicts with the Greek philosophical heritage
influential in Arianism, and Athanasius is incapable of resolving
the intellectual dilemma that this conflict creates. Arian logic
compelled them to believe that the Word could not be fully divine
because of the Incarnation and crucifixion. In spite of holding to
full divinity, Athanasius retains the image of divine condescension as does tradition after him. Others follow with better explanations, however. Gregory of Nyssa and Didymus the Blind, or
one of his pupils, discover new theological possibilities and develop more positive understandings of mutability, Gregory on the
human, pseudo-Didymus on the divine level.

GREGORY OF NYSSA

If the fourth century is one of strong reaction to opposing christological views, it is also and perhaps more importantly the time

---

[38] Ibid., 256B.

[39] Ibid., 277C. This passage is ambiguous and may refer to creation. See J.
Roldanus, *Le Christ et L'Homme dans la Theologie D'Athanase D'Alexandrie* (Leiden:
Brill, 1977), 200–201; 211–12. I take it to refer to Incarnation because of *adelphos*,
however. In 284A–B the lowering refers to both creation and Incarnation.

[40] *De Inc.*, 46.3.

[41] *Philanthrōpia* in *De Inc.* 8.5.

[42] Ibid., 8.14.

[43] *Disc.* 4, 516C in PG 26. It contains two important words, *philanthrōpon* and
synkatabasin. This text is non-Athanasian however.

when the Incarnation made its deepest impression on Christian theological writing. New philosophical concepts and language are created to accommodate belief in the Incarnation and in the Trinity of persons. Gregory of Nyssa (c. 330–395) is one of the most important contributors to reflection in both areas. And more importantly here, he takes mutability more seriously, at least on the created level, than anyone before him.

Gregory uses all the Greek terms for immutability interchangeably to distinguish God from creatures. He writes:

> The uncreated nature is incapable of admitting of such movement (*kinēsis*) as is implied in turning (*metabolē*) or change (*tropē*) or alteration (*alloiōsis*), while everything that subsists through creation has connection with change (*alloiōsis*), inasmuch as the subsistence itself of the creation had its rise in change (*alloiōsis*).[44]

Immutability is the primary attribute of God in *The Life of Moses* 2.25. God is true being, "which is always the same, neither increasing nor diminishing, immutable to all change whether to better or to worse . . . standing in need of nothing else, alone desireable."[45]

Belief in God's immutability has an ethical side as well. In a passage he wrote against the neo-Arian Eunomius, Gregory connects faith in the unchangeable uncreated Trinity with the attainment of a "steadfast unalterable life" rather than a changeable one in which we are "tossed about by the waves of this lifetime of uncertainty and change."[46]

Gregory argues on the other hand that unless there is change in us, there would be no characteristic to distinguish us from God in whose image we are made: "Alteration (*tropē*) is necessarily

---

[44] *Cat. Or.* 6, in James H. Srawley, *The Catechetical Oration of Gregory of Nyssa* (Cambridge: University Press, 1956), 33–34.

[45] I use the translation of Abraham J. Malherbe and Everett Ferguson, *Life of Moses* (New York: Paulist, 1978). For Greek text see J. Danielou's edition in SC 1, 3rd ed., (Paris: Cerf. 1968), 60.

[46] *Cat. Or.* 39 in Srawley, 156.

observable in man . . . because man was an imitation of the divine nature, and unless some distinctive difference had been occasioned, the imitating subject would be entirely the same as that which it resembles."[47] Although created nature resembles the divine, "The uncreated nature is . . . immutable (*atrepton*) and always remains the same while the created nature cannot exist without change (*alloiōseos*)."[48]

In spite of the fact that God is radically distinguished from creatures because of divine immutability, Gregory believes that human change, if it is progress in perfection, is a positive characteristic. This novel idea has impressed a number of important scholars, especially Jean Danielou; it is Gregory's distinctive contribution to Christian anthropology. In one of his homilies on the *Song of Songs,* Gregory says: "First there is the uncreated substance, itself the Creator of all things, that remains eternally what it is. Remaining ever unchangeable it transcends all addition or diminution; it cannot receive any further perfection."[49]

Mutability is the distinguishing feature of creation. The world "is constantly being created, ever changing for the better in its growth in perfection." In this process "no limit can be envisaged, nor can its progressive growth in perfection be limited by any term. In this way, its present state of perfection, no matter how great and perfect it might be, is merely the beginning of a greater and superior stage." This growth in perfection is not

---

[47] *Cat. Or.* 21 in ibid., p. 81. Discussions of immutability in Gregory include Jean Danielou's Introduction to *From Glory to Glory* (New York: Scribner's Sons, 1961), 48f; "Le probleme du changement chez Grégoire de Nysse," *Archives de philosophie* 29 (1966): 323–47. This article is reprinted in his *L'Etre et le temps chez Grégoire de Nysse* (Leiden: Brill, 1970), 95–115; E. Ferguson, "God's Infinity and Man's Mutability: Perpetual Progress According to Gregory of Nyssa," *Greek Orthodox Theological Review* 18 (1973): 57–78; Ronald E. Heine, *Perfection in the Virtuous Life: A Study in the Relationship Between Edification and Polemical Theology in Gregory of Nyssa's De Vita Moysis,* Patristic Monograph Series 2 (Cambridge: Philadelphia Patristic Foundation, 1975), 46–61.

[48] *De op. hom.* 16.12, 184C in PG 44; also *Contra Eunomium* (hereafter CE) 3.2.10 in Werner Jaeger, ed., *Gregorii Nysseni Opera* (Leiden: Brill, 1952f.), 2, 55. I will refer to the several volumes in this edition as GNO; see also *Vit. Mos.* 2.2f.

[49] *Comm. in Cant.* 6. GNO 6.174.8f.; Danielou, *From Glory to Glory,* 196–197.

automatic, and although change for the worse is always possible, the Word is a pedagogue or a guardian protecting us from change for the worse:

> Though we are changeable by nature, the Word wants us never to change for the worse; but by constant progress in perfection, we are to make our mutability an aid in our rise towards higher things, and by the very changeability of our nature to establish it immovably in good.[50]

The reason for human mutability is endless progress in perfection. At the end of Gregory's treatise on perfection, he eloquently states this remarkable idea, sounding virtually modern:

> Therefore I do not think it is a fearful thing, I mean that our nature is changeable (*treptēn*). The Logos shows that it would be a disadvantage for us not to be able to make a change (*alloiōsin*) for the better, as a kind of wing of flight to greater things. Therefore, let no one be grieved if he sees in his nature a penchant for change (*metabolēn*). Changing (*alloioumenos*) in everything for the better, let him exchange "glory for glory" becoming greater through daily increase.[51]

The limitlessness or infinity of God parallels human mutability,[52] and Gregory associates God's infinity with divine incomprehensibility. "The characteristic of the divine nature is to transcend all characteristics." God is true being, "inaccessible to knowledge . . . infinite, enclosed by no boundary," so God can never be entirely seen:[53] "This truly is the vision of God; never to be satisfied in the desire to see him. But one must always, by looking at what

---

[50] *Comm. in Cant.* 8. GNO 6.252.9f.; Danielou, *From Glory to Glory,* 216.

[51] *De Perfectione* GNO 8.1.213.20–214.4.

[52] E. Mühlenberg, *Die Unendlichkeit Göttes bei Gregor von Nyssa* (Göttingen: Vandenhoeck & Ruprecht, 1966); "Die philosophische Bildung Gregors von Nyssa in den Buchen *Contra Eunomium,*" in *Ecriture Et Culture Philosophique Dan Le Pensée De Grégoire De Nysse,* ed. M. Harl (Leiden: Brill, 1971), 230–51; Robert S. Brightman, "Apophatic Theology and Divine Infinity in St. Gregory of Nyssa," *The Greek Orthodox Theological Review* 18 (1973): 97–114.

[53] *Vit. Mos.* 2.234–36; 2.162.

he can see, rekindle his desire to see more. Thus no limit would interrupt growth in the ascent to God."[54]

Gregory's positive understanding of human mutability does not carry over into his understanding of God because it is precisely immutability that distinguishes God from creatures. Nevertheless, there is evidence that Gregory tried to adjust this philosophical understanding of God to belief in the Incarnation, specifically in passages dealing with the divine kenosis.

APATHEIA

In most places in his work, Gregory tends to use *apatheia* in reference to all feelings and to exalt the Christian attempt to attain it. *Apatheia* in its usual meaning is the absence of all the passions, and Gregory inherits this usage.[55] At times, however, he does give a positive evaluation of some human emotions: "It is necessary that desire (*epithymian*) be founded on the purity of the soul. . . . Anger and rage and hatred should be aroused, like dogs guarding gates, only for resistance to sin."[56] In the sixth homily on the beatitudes, wrath is not completely forbidden. "For sometimes one may lawfully turn such an emotion also to good use. . . . The use of anger is often opportune, namely, whenever this passion is roused for the chastisement of sin."[57]

There is yet another interesting feature of Gregory's understanding of *apatheia*. He sometimes states that one ought to strive for it in imitation of the divine. At other times, he argues that the attainment of *apatheia* is impossible for material beings. Two texts on the beatitudes express this well. According to Gregory, God

---

[54] Ibid., 2.239.

[55] Ibid., 2.303; *Cat. Or.* 35; 6.8. See the text cited by Walter Völker, *Gregor Von Nyssa Als Mystiker* (Wiesbaden: Franz Steiner, 1955), 259–64. He accepts the dictum that "Die Apathielehre ist von zentraler Bedeutung in der Bildtheologie Gregors." 259.

[56] *De Virginitate* 18.2.16. See Michael Abineau's Introduction to *Traité de la Virginité* SC 119 (Paris: Cerf, 1966), 166–71.

[57] PG 44, 1276A.

does not call blessed those who live in complete isolation from the passions. Meekness, however, which is a feature of the incarnate Word, is possible and suffices for earthly beatitude, and for this reason, blessed are the meek.[58]

Gregory writes, "The end of the life of virtue is to become like to God. Yet man can by no means whatever imitate the purity that is without passion." He then says that we must be able to imitate God in some way in order to achieve beatitude. We can imitate the voluntary humility of the incarnate Word, since humility befits our earthly condition. In this passage the kenosis of the divine Word becomes the key for *homoiōsis Theou*, the imitation of God.[59]

THE INCARNATION

One of Eunomius's arguments against the divinity of the Word is that Jesus suffered and died on the Cross, while the divine is impassible. Gregory states a principle reminiscent of the *Ad Theopompum*, as is this entire text: "Nothing is truly passion which does not tend to sin."[60] He then distinguishes between *pathos* and *ergon*, arguing that *pathos* is used improperly if it is applied to sinless desires, such as pain or fear of death. The *apatheia* of the Lord refers to divine sinlessness, not to divine impassibility in an absolute sense.[61] In other words, the impassibility of the Logos does not mean that the Logos did not suffer in any sense whatever. It only means that the divine cannot sin.

---

[58] Ibid., 1216B. Norris believes that Gregory is two-minded about *apatheia*. Is pathos "a natural part of man's God-given constitution" for him or a "perversion of this nature, i.e., vice?" For Norris, Gregory's position "reflects, in its very difficulties and apparent confusions, the logic of late Platonic speculation on the impassibility of the soul." See R. A. Norris, *Manhood and Christ: A Study in the Christology of Theodore of Mopsuestia* (Oxford: Clarendon, 1963), 34–35 n. 4. Also Jean Danielou, *Platonisme et Théologie Mystique* (Paris: Aubier, 1944), 99–110; Jerome Gaith, *La Conception de la Liberté chez Grégoire de Nysse* (Paris: J. Vrin, 1953), 60–63.

[59] PG 44, 1200C.

[60] CE 3.4.27, GNO 2.144. The same argument is in *Or. Cat.* 16.

[61] For *apatheia* of the divine nature in the generation of the Word see CE 3.2.58f., GNO 2.71.

Gregory's understanding of *pathos* here is christological. He defines *pathos* as sinful desire in order to hold with the tradition that God is without *pathos*. The Incarnation does not take away the human feelings of Jesus. Even more importantly, it is an act of divine philanthropy, an act in which both the Father and Son share. This philanthropy is certainly a passion. To say that God is *apathēs* means only that unruly disordered passions have no place in the divine, but it is not to exempt God, as Origen put it, from the passion of love. The Incarnation is the supreme example of this passion.

The Life of Moses 2.28–30 suggests that the Logos changed in the Incarnation. Exodus 4:1–9 provides the context, the story of the two signs given to Moses that he was the Lord's appointed. The second sign is the instantaneous contraction of leprosy on Moses' hand after placing it in his bosom. His hand is cured by repeating the same action. This passage leads Gregory to reflect on Ps. 76:11, which he interprets christologically. He writes, "Although the divine nature is contemplated in its immutability (*annalloiōto*), by condescension to the weakness of human nature it was changed (*alloiōtheisēs*) to our shape and form (*schēma te kai eidos*)."[62]

Returning to Exodus, Gregory suggests that the bosom of Moses signifies the bosom of the Father and the hand of Moses is the Logos. Thus "when he was manifested to us from the bosom of the Father, he was changed to be like us." This was not the final change of the Word however. "After he wiped away our infirmities, he again returned to his own bosom the hand which had been among us and had received our complexion. (The Father is the bosom of the right hand.)" Gregory's final comment attempts to preserve the divine immutability by assigning change to the human nature of Jesus.

What is impassible by nature (*apathes tēs physeōs*) did not change (*ēlloiōsin*) into what is passible, but what is mutable and subject to

---

[62] 2.28, in Malherbe and Ferguson, *Life of Moses*, 61.

passions (*to trepton te kai empathes*) was transformed into impassibility through its participation in the immutable (*atrepton*).[63]

It seems arbitrary to associate change only with the human nature of Jesus rather than the divine. Divine kenosis suggests that the Logos changes. Is this equivalent to a denial of the divinity of the Word as in Arianism? Or is there another alternative, dimly perceived by Gregory because of his positive attitude toward change?[64]

In his polemic against Eunomius, Gregory argues that the divinity and consequent immutability of the Logos is necessary. Without them, there would be no divine condescension, no kenosis. If this is lost, the essential mystery of faith, faith in the elevation of the human through the emptying of the divine, goes with it.

> And this we declare to be the mystery of the Lord according to the flesh, that He who is immutable (*atreptos*) came to be in that which is mutable and to that end altering it for the better, and changing it from the worse.[65]

Gregory then describes Eunomius's understanding of the Incarnation:

> He, being Himself created, came to that which was kindred and homogeneous with Himself, not coming from a transcendent nature to put on the lowlier nature by reason of his love to man, but becoming that very thing which He was.

The Arian view of Incarnation brings no salvation because there is no master mingling with servants, but only a servant with other servants. Gregory's own language of Incarnation and consequent elevation of human nature is very strong. "But the flesh

---

[63] 2.30, in ibid., 62.

[64] See J. R. Bouchet, "La vocabulaire de l'union et du rapport des natures chez saint Grégoire de Nysse," *Revue Thomiste* 68 (1968): 565. Also the discussion of Ps. 76:11 in CE 3.4.25, GNO 2.143.

[65] CE 3.3.52, GNO 2.126; CE 3.2.39, GNO 2.65 for a denial that the Logos changes.

was not identical with the Godhead, till this too was transformed to the Godhead."[66] Human nature mingles with the divine so that it becomes divine. "The Godhead empties Itself that it may come within the capacity of the human nature, and the human nature is renewed by becoming divine through its commixture with the divine."[67] But there is no divine suffering as a result of the Incarnation. God's lowering does not pollute God's nature, but does divinize the humanity of Jesus in an important sense.[68]

Thus although Gregory is committed to the philosophical idea of divine immutability, he also believes in the progressive realization of human spiritual perfection and in the importance of human feelings. This shows him how religiously important our capacity for change and our passions are, which is something new for patristic theology. Even though Gregory does not attribute mutability or feeling to God, he does have a positive view of change and passion on the anthropological level. And most importantly, like Athanasius before him, he is deeply impressed by the divine condescension of the Logos in the Incarnation. It means that God suffered in some sense. Although Gregory suggests that a historical Incarnation implies change and passion on God's part, he does not construct a systematic understanding of divine mutability or passibility to accommodate his intuition. A fourth-century Alexandrian author in a commentary on the Psalms borrows terminology from Aristotle to attempt this.

THE COMMENTARY ON THE PSALMS
FROM TURA

The author of the *Commentary on the Psalms* discovered at Tura used the term *alloiōsis* to describe the divine kenosis in the Incarnation, insisting that change belonged not only to the humanity

---

[66] CE 3.3.62f., GNO 2.130.

[67] CE 3.3.67, GNO 2.131; also 3.4.43, GNO 2.150; for a brief, accurate presentation of the manner of union, see J. N. D. Kelly, *Early Christian Doctrines*, 298–300.

[68] CE 3.4.1f., GNO 2.134f.; also CE 3.14.17, GNO 2.140.

of Jesus but to the divine Logos as well. This recently discovered commentary presents a Christology that is a turning point in the tradition. If we can appropriately conceptualize the divine manner of change, we can present divine incarnation in a reasonable manner, without rejecting it by lowering the level of the Word as the Arians did, and without affirming it paradoxically as Athanasius did. Arius had argued that precisely the mutable and passible nature of the Word determined that it was not and could not be divine. Athanasius agreed that indeed, if Arius was correct about the Word's mutability, Arius's conclusion was likewise correct. But for Athanasius, the Logos was immutable, *analloiōtos* and *atreptos*, therefore divine. Only Jesus could change.

Philo had never used the term *analloiōtos* for God in spite of clear philosophical precedent; neither is God called *apathēs*. Both Clement and Origen use both terms for God and for the Word, although they vacillate in some passages. Clement writes of God "condescending to emotion on man's account; for whose sake also the Word of God became man."[69] And in one of his homilies Origen says that both the Father and the Logos suffer from the passion of love for us.[70] There is also the *Ad Theopompum* of Pseudo-Gregory the Wonderworker, which attempts to work out a logic of divine suffering, and Gregory of Nyssa's contribution, which we saw above.

Who is the author of this commentary? The usual answer is Didymus the Blind (c. 313–398), the famous pupil of Origen. The question of the authorship of works ascribed to Didymus, however, is difficult. That he wrote the *De Trinitate* has been challenged since 1957.[71] Reynolds argues convincingly that the *Commentary on Ezechiel* and the *Commentary on the Psalms* have essentially the same Christology, but does not notice that they

---

[69] *Paedagogus* 1.8.62 in GCS 1, 133.

[70] *Hom. in Ezech.* 6.6 in GCS 8.384–85.

[71] L. Doutreleau, "Le *De Trinitate* est-il l'oeuvre de Didyme l'Aveugle?" *Recherches de science religieuse* 45 (1957): 514–57. For a complete discussion of the state of the question up to 1972, see A. Heron, *Studies in the Trinitarian Writings of Didymus the Blind: His Authorship of the Adversus Eunomius IV–V and the De Trinitate* (Tübingen: Diss., 1972), 1–10. This work contains very little on the question of divine immutability (155–57) and nothing on the use of *alloiōsis* in the *Commentary on the Psalms*.

vary at a crucial point. Only the latter proposes that in the Incarnation the Word changes.[72] Bienert calls the commentary one of two "Kollegnachschriften" allowing for the authorship of an anonymous disciple of Didymus.[73] For my purposes the question of authorship is of slight importance. The author or authors of all the works attributed to Didymus, with the exception of the *Commentary on the Psalms*, has or have virtually the same understanding of divine emotions and immutability as that of Origen, the standard Alexandrian view that both are impossible.[74]

The terminological contribution of the *Commentary* has been available because of the work of A. Gesché since the early 1960s, but theology has yet to appreciate its full significance.[75] Gesché affirmed the importance of the human soul of Jesus in the *Commentary* but viewed the teaching about divine mutability with some suspicion.[76] The *Commentary* departed from the tradition's fairly unanimous teaching that the Word became flesh while remaining immutable and impassible, and for good reason. The

---

[72] S. C. Reynolds, *Man, Incarnation, and Trinity in the Commentary on Zechariah of Didymus the Blind of Alexandria* (Ph.D. diss., Harvard University, 1966), chap. 3, p. 36f.

[73] W. Bienert, *"Allegoria" und "Anagoge" Bei Didymos Dem Blinde Von Alexandria* (Berlin: W. de Gruyter, 1972), 5–31. The other is the *Commentary on Ecclesiastes*.

[74] Jürgen Hönsheid, *Didymus der Blinde De Trinitate* Buch 1 (Mesenheim am Glan: Anton Hain, 1975), 1.14 (p. 40) paralleled exactly in *Ps. Athan.* 1180C–1181A, PG 28. Also Hönsheid, *Didymus* 1.74 (p. 166); 1.71 (160); but see 1.33 (78–79): "He who is impassible (*apathēs*) became passible (*epathen*) for us."; 1.24 (58); 1.9 (32); for *De Spiritu Sancto* 1036, 1041, 1044–45, 1083–84 in PG 39; *Kata Manichaion* 1088 & 1104 in ibid.; *In Zach.* 5.35, p. 986 in SC 85; 1.10, p. 194 in SC 83; 2.192f., p. 515f. in SC 84.

[75] My discussion is heavily indebted to his work. A. Gesché, *La Christologie du "Commentaire sur les Psaumes" découvert à Toura* (Gembloux: J. Duculot, 1962); "L'âme humaine de Jésus dans la Christologie du IVème s. le témoignage du Commentaire sur les Psaumes découvert à Toura," *Revue d'histoire ecclésiastique* 54 (1959): 385–425. In this article he discusses the unique concept of the *propatheia* of Jesus' human soul. See also A. Grillmeier, *Christ in the Christian Tradition* 1: 363f. For *propatheia* as a creative answer to Apollinaris's lack of a doctrine of Jesus' human soul, see L. Koenen and R. Merklebach, *Didymos der Blinde: Kommentar zum Ecclesiastes Teil 4* (Bonn: R. Habelt, 1972), 157–58. Other discussions of the Tura manuscripts include L. Doutreleau and L. Koenen, "Nouvel inventaire des Papyrus de Toura," *Recherches de science religieuse* 55 (1967): 547–64; L. Doutreleau, "Que savons-nous aujourd'hui des papyrus de Toura?" in ibid., 43 (1955): 161–93.

[76] At one point he wonders if the term *alloiōsis* is a "mot dangereux" when applied to the Incarnation. (*La Christologie*, 243). The general tone of his discussion is a defense of the author against possible charges of unorthodoxy.

author wanted to improve upon it by distinguishing among various types of change to argue that one type was appropriate to the divine case.

There are some general discussions of *alloiōsis* in the *Commentary*, which will lead us to the application of this term to the Logos in the Incarnation. The first verses of two psalms in the Septuagint, Ps. 33:1 and 44:1, have the term. In the *Commentary* there is also a discussion of *alloiōsis* at Ps. 20:1 whose context is unclear, since this verse does not have the word at least in the Septuagint. "From Scripture and natural insight we suppose about God that God is *atreptos* and *analloiōtos* since whatever has no underlying quality neither changes nor alters (*trepetai, alloioutai*)."[77]

The author then makes a case for distinguishing *atreptos* from *analloiōtos* by describing the special nature of *alloiōsis* as a distinct type of change which is different from changes of becoming or of growth. *Alloiōsis*, is a *metabolē kata poion*, a change of quality. Two examples of this type of change are movements from vice to virtue and from sickness to health. Other changes and movements such as becoming and growth are not changes of quality, but of being or of quantity. *Alloiōsis* means a distinctive type of change, not the same as any other type. Hence *alloiōsis* is no synonym for *atreptos*. The theological context of this passage is a critique of anthropomorphisms,[78] and a christological statement of belief in the God-man.

At Ps. 44:1, the author gives four distinct types of *metabolē* or *kinēsis*: (1) change of becoming, for instance, egg to bird; seed to corn; (2) change of corruption, for example, corruption of the human body; (3) change of growth, for example, from smaller to larger, or larger to smaller, implying perishing; (4) change of quality (*poion*), which is *alloiōsis*.[79]

In the distinction between *atreptos* and *analloiōtos*, Gesché discovered the influence of Aristotle's *Physics*. In that work,

---

[77] The edition of the *Commentary* is the five volumes of Didymos der Blinde, *Psalmenkommentar* (*Tura Papyrus*) in *Papyrologische Texte und Abhandlungen,* ed. L. Doutreleau, A. Gesché, and M. Grönewald (Bonne: R. Habelt, 1968 and years following). This text is in v.1, p. 2.

[78] v.14, p. 8.

[79] v.5, p. 184f. See Gesché, *La Christologie,* 232–40.

Aristotle distinguishes four types of *metabolē* or *kinēsis:* (1) change of being, either becoming or corruption; (2) change of quantity, either growth or perishing; (3) change of place, that is, motion; (4) change of quality (*poion*), which is *alloiōsis.* [80]

There are obvious differences between the distinctions of the *Commentary* and those of Aristotle, but the similarities are also pronounced. The *Commentary* follows the Aristotle of *Physics* 200b in using *metabolē* and *kinēsis* synonymously. In other places in the same work, Aristotle distinguished them, arguing that coming into being and corruption are instances of change but not of motion.[81] The following are instances of qualitative change for the *Commentary:* sickness to health, ignorance to knowledge, unbelief to belief, vice to virtue and virtue to vice.[82] An eschatologically perfect realization of the qualities of knowledge, virtue, wisdom, and holiness is also called an *alloiōsis.*[83] I suspect the change of quality that the *Commentary* has in mind for the Incarnation is the change of shape or form (*morphē*) from Aristotle, since Phil. 2 has that very word.

THE INCARNATION

The author of the *Commentary* applies the term *alloiōsis* to the Incarnation because of a christological interpretation of the word in the first verse of Psalm 33 and Psalm 44. In both cases the word reminds him of Ps. 76:11, the controlling passage for his use of *alloiōsis.*

---

[80] 200b, 34f. See chapter 1 above.

[81] *Phys.* 192b, 15f and 225b, 8–9. Also *Phys.* 243a, 9–10 where three types of *kinēsis* are mentioned, movement of place, quantity, and quality. 224a, 21f.; 241a, 32.

[82] Ps. 20:1, v.1, p. 2. The beginning of the *Commentary on Job* distinguishes between two types of change, one that is physical, and one that is freely chosen, as from good to evil. That *Commentary* makes this distinction in order to argue that the devil in Job was a fallen angel, fallen by choice and was not made evil. See Albert Henrichs, *Didymus Der Blinde. Kommentar Zu Hiob*, in *Papyrologische Texte Und Abhandlungen*, B.1 (Bonn: R. Habelt, 1968), 26–28.

[83] Ps. 44:1. See Gesché, *La Christologie*, 235–40 for a discussion of the use of *alloiōsis* in the eschatology of the *Commentary.*

In the *Septuagint* Ps. 33:1 reads: "A psalm of David, when he
altered his face before Abimelech; and he let him go, and he departed." The *ēlloiōsen* in reference to David's face suggests that
the change was voluntary. This is a *metabolē poiotētos,* or qualitative change, and brings to mind another *alloiōsis,* the alteration of
the face of the Savior in the assumption of the form of a slave.[84]
The alteration is not a *metabolē* from one form into another, but a
concealment (*epikrypsis*) of one form in another that is visible.

The *Commentary* states the principle that is all important for
distinguishing the type of change appropriate to the Incarnation.
It states unequivocally, "Alteration (*alloiōsis*) of the face (*prosōpou*)
of the unchanging (*atreptou*) can occur." This alteration brings Ps.
76:11 to mind. In a comment on Ps. 76:11 in the Septuagint,
which reads "And I said, now I have begun, this is the alteration of
the right hand of the Most High," the *Commentary* says, "The right
hand of the Most High is *atreptos* and *analloiōtos,*" thereby giving
a nod to tradition. But the Word does change in some sense:
"Eternally it is identical and the same. We do not mean anyone
other than the Savior. How then does He change do we think? He
descends to educate. For we are truly aided if he descends."[85] The
right hand of God refers often to the Savior who altered Himself
to become flesh, a curse. He took it upon himself to become sin so
that the sins (of the human race) might become God's justice in
him.[86]

However this important passage is translated into English,
its force should not be weakened. God came to be enfleshed in a
real way, and for the *Commentary* this indicates that some type of
real alteration took place in God, specifically a change of quality,
the quality of form (*morphē*). This alteration, the text continues, is
a *proslēpsis,* an addition, or a "taking-to-oneself," not a transformation (*metabolē*). "The Logos became flesh and took the form of

---

[84] v. 3: 202: *alloiōsin tou prosōpou tou sōtēros.*

[85] *synkatabainei paideusa.* v. 5: 188. Of interest are parallels for the exegesis of
Ps. 44:1 and 76:11b contained in Ekkehard Mühlenberg, *Psalmenkommentare Aus
Der Katenüberlieferung* (Berlin: Walter de Gruyter, 1975–77), 1: 335; 2: 122–3.

[86] Compare the translation of Gesché, *La Christologie,* p. 244, with the stronger
version of Grönewald, *Psalmenkommentar,* v. 3, p. 203.

a slave, altered himself not by a transformation as I have often said, but by addition."[87]

It seems clear that the term *proslēpsis* is used here to indicate the specific type of divine alteration which occurred in the Incarnation. In describing how the Logos changed, the author used Aristotle's distinctions. More deeply, however, the *Commentary* uses Aristotle in a specifically Christian manner. For Aristotle, there are alterations of qualities in the world at large, but never in the divine. For the *Commentary* the Incarnation is an alteration of the divine Logos, a change of form or a taking-to-oneself without loss of the divine essence.

Psalm 44:1 says: "For the end, for alternate (*alloiōthēsou-menōn*) strains by the sons of Core; for instruction, a Song concerning the beloved." The term *alloiōthēsoumenōn* again brings Ps. 76:11 to mind. As mentioned previously, the *Commentary* disagrees with the patristic teaching which views *atreptos* and *analloiōtos* as synonyms. Although the right hand of God has both attributes, it is *alloiōtos* according to the economy of salvation, that is, because of its enfleshment.[88]

Thus the *Commentary* uses three different phrases to express the qualitative alteration of the Word of God in the Incarnation. It is an alteration of form by which the divine invisible form is hidden in the human and visible manifestation; it is an addition to the divine self, or a taking-to-itself of the human; it is an alteration for the sake of the economy of salvation, an enfleshment.

Gesché has briefly examined various patristic texts to see whether any parallels can be found for the *Commentary*'s use of *alloiōsis* for the Logos in the Incarnation.[89] Since there is no complete study of the uses of this term in the tradition, no certain conclusion can be drawn on this question. A look at several different interpretations of the three relevant psalm verses leads to some interesting discoveries however. Only two passages are truly parallel, one from Origen, and one whose authorship is

---

[87] Ibid., p. 204: *ou kata metabolēn . . . alla kata proslēpsin.*
[88] Ibid., 5: 192: *ouk alloiōtheis kata tēn theotēta, alla kata tēn oikonomian, kata tēn enanthrōpēsin.*
[89] Gesché, *La Christologie*, p. 252–60.

problematic. The Origen passage is an exegesis of Ps. 76:11, which
states, "The right hand of the Most High is the Savior who altered
himself, taking the form of a slave."[90] This is followed by a comment in reference to the effect of the Incarnation, clearly echoed in
the *Psalm Commentary*. The Incarnation results in another, soteriological alteration according to Origen. It is a restoration from mal-
ice and ignorance to virtue and knowledge.[91]

The Origen text is of special importance because it suggests
that the author of the *Commentary* perhaps owes inspiration entirely to Origen, whose exegesis of Ps. 76:11 led him to apply
Aristotle's analysis of change to the change of the Logos in the
Incarnation. Whether this is true or not, the *Commentary* certainly
tries to do justice to the fact that the Incarnation of God's Word
makes a real difference to God. It stands virtually alone in the late
fourth century with this important contribution. Gesché's statement that these texts do nothing but express a "fidélité au vocabulaire biblique"[92] misses the point. Linguistic fidelity to biblical
vocabulary indicates a willingness to challenge the prevailing
philosophical fidelity that made synonyms of *atreptos* and *analloiōtos*. The idea that God changes in the Incarnation comes from
the dynamic Christology of the Alexandrian school, with its sense
of the unity of God and Jesus, and its insistence that God truly
suffered in Him.

---

[90] PG 12, 1540B: *ēlloiōsen eauton, morphēn doulou labōn.*

[91] The second passage says: "The Only-Begotten is said to be altered, not by a
metabolē but by a *proslēpsis.*" PG 69, 1192. A parallel is in Gregory's *Life of Moses*
2.28. In 2.30 Gregory makes it clear that the alteration is only on our part,
however, not on the part of God who is *atreptos kai apathēs*. In his exegesis of
Ps. 44:1, Eusebius points out (in a corrective way?) that so far as the Word is God,
he is both *analloiōtos kai atreptos*. PG 23, 392B. For others who interpret simi-
larly, see Gesché, *La Christologie,* 256–60.

[92] Ibid., 260.

5

GOD IN THE FORM OF A SLAVE

Hilary of Poitiers and St. Augustine

The issue of divine immutability and impassibility became important in the fourth century because of Arianism. If the Logos was changeable by nature and capable of suffering, it could not have divine status. Out of the Alexandrian response to Arius, only one author, Didymus the Blind or his pupil, suggested a linguistic and theological solution, the seeds of which were already contained in Origen, the *Ad Theopompum*, Athanasius, and Gregory of Nyssa. The *Commentary on the Psalms* from Tura developed a notion of change derived from Aristotle which preserves the divinity of God's Word. In using the term *alloiōsis* for the change of the Logos in the act of Incarnation, one is able to say that the Word truly becomes flesh without losing the divine nature.

HILARY OF POITIERS

Such is not the case with Hilary of Poitiers (d. 367). Hilary argues many times that the Logos is both unchangeable and impassible:

> For he was able to suffer, and yet the Word was not passible. Passibility denotes a nature that is weak; but suffering in itself is

101

the endurance of pains inflicted, and since the Godhead is immutable and yet the Word was made flesh, such pains found in
Him a material which they could affect though the person of the
Word had no infirmity or passibility. And so when he suffered his
nature remained immutable, because like his Father, his person is
of an impassible essence, though it is born.[1]

This view appears several times in the *De Trinitate:* "God, I am
sure, is subject to no change. His eternity admits not of defect or
amendment, of gain or of loss."[2] In a discussion of the *homoousion*
and of divine generation, Hilary connects immutability and impassibility: "God, being impassible, cannot be divided, for, if he
must submit to be lessened by division, he is subject to change,
and will be rendered imperfect if his perfect substance leave him
to reside in the severed portion."[3]

For Hilary there is no wavering on this point; he has absorbed the tradition completely. Yet several of his christological
texts show an inconsistency as to the interpretation of Phil 2:6–8,
the kenotic hymn that is so important in the Christology of the
fourth century. Recall what an impact it had on the author of
the *Commentary.* Hilary not only defends the divine unchanging
nature of the Word against the Arians. He tries to develop a
theology of divine kenosis as well, inconsistent though this dual
aim appears.[4]

Hilary develops his understanding of the divine kenosis and
his exegesis of Phil. 2:6–8 by attending to the terms *"forma dei"*
and *"forma servi."* In many passages of *De Trinitate* he argues that
a real *evacuatio* of the divine *forma* took place in Jesus: "He emptied himself of the form of God, that is, of that wherein He was

---

[1] *De Synodis* 49, in PL 10. 516B–517A.

[2] *De Trinitate* 3.13, in CCL 62.84, lines 2–4.

[3] Ibid., 4.4.104, lines 25–28. See also 3.15; 3.16; 4.8; 5.17; 5.34; 6.2; 6.17; 10.2; 11.47.

[4] For a historical summary of kenotic Christology, see the comprehensive article by P. Henry, "Kénose," *Dictionnaire de la Bible Supplément* (Paris: Letouzey et Ané, 1957), 5: 7–161.

equal with God."[5] It is clear that the two *formae* do not coexist. Hilary states:

> The obedience of death has nothing to do with the form of God, just as the form of God is not inherent in the form of a servant . . . nor could He who was abiding in the form of God, take the form of a servant without emptying himself, since the combination of the two forms would be disharmonious.[6]

In spite of the loss of the *forma dei*, the divine nature remains, so that Jesus remains divine. Hilary writes: "The Incarnation is summed up in this, that the whole son, that is his manhood as well as his divinity, was permitted by the Father's gracious favor to continue in the unity of the Father's nature."[7] The divine nature did not cease to exist but was "exercising its proper power in the fashion of the humility it assumed."[8]

Hilary's interpretation of Phil. 2:6–8 leads him to distinguish between the divine form and nature, holding that the former is left behind in the Incarnation, while the latter is preserved. And, of course, this implies some type of divine mutability. But Hilary is not consistent on this point. In *De Trinitate* 10.22, he reverses his position and argues from that point on that the two forms, that of God and of servant, could and indeed did coexist. From 10.22 on, there is no distinction between *forma* and *natura* at all: "Thus it was just as true, that he received the form of a slave, as that he remained in the form of God. The use of the word 'form' to describe both natures compels us to recognize that he truly possessed both."[9] Hilary is adamant about this reversal. In 10.22 he seems to have suddenly grasped the importance of the issue. Distinguishing between the two forms invites reflection, which without the distinction that Didymus made, could lead to a denial

---

[5] "Exinavit autem se ex Dei forma, id est ex eo quod aequalis Deo erat." *De Trin.*, 8.45, in CCL 62A, 358, 17.

[6] *De Trin.* 9.14, in ibid., 385. Disharmonious = "non conveniente sibi."

[7] *De Trin.* 9.38, in ibid., 412, 11, "per indulgentiam paternae voluntatis."

[8] *De Trin.* 9.51, in ibid., 429, 28–29. Also 10.7; 10.15, 19, 20.

[9] *De Trin.* 10.22, in ibid., 476, 24–27.

of divine immutability, hence of the divinity of the Word. If so, Hilary would have fallen into the hands of his Arian opponents.

This reversal on the use of *forma dei* is coupled with Hilary's somewhat docetic comments about the divinized humanity of Jesus. For example:

> So the man Jesus Christ, only-begotten God, as flesh and as Word at the same time Son of Man and Son of God, without ceasing to be himself, that is, God, took true humanity after the likeness of our humanity. But when, in this humanity, he was struck with blows, or smitten with wounds, or bound with ropes, or lifted on high, he felt the force of suffering, but without its pain (10.23).[10]

Although Jesus' body was human, it could not feel pain.[11] He ate and drank, not out of necessity, but as a concession to us.[12]

These comments are the occasion of much scholarly interest.[13] Galtier explains the inconsistent use of *forma* by distinguishing two senses, a broad one and a narrow one, in which Hilary uses the term. In the proper narrow sense of *forma dei* as glory and majesty, there can be no coexistence with the *forma servi.* But in the broad sense the two can coexist.[14] Yet Galtier does not notice the connection in the text of *De Trinitate* between the shift away from the first narrow meaning of *forma dei* as a state of divine being which was set aside, to the second meaning, in which the divine and human form can coexist, and how this shift results in Hilary's divinizing of the humanity of Jesus. The shift of meaning and the docetic comments not only occur together, but are obviously related. As soon as the divine *forma* and *natura* become equivalent in 10.22, the divine *forma* begins to overshadow the

---

[10] "Ineptum passionis, non tamen dolorem passionis inferrent," in ibid., 477, 1–7.

[11] *De Trin.* 10.23.

[12] Ibid., 10.24. Also 10.28, 35, 44.

[13] See the summary of literature on this up to 1966 in C. F. A. Borchardt, *Hilary of Poitiers' Role in the Arian Struggle* (Hague: M. Nijhoff, 1966), 117–30; also Paul Galtier, *Saint Hilaire De Poitiers* (Paris: Beauchesne, 1960), 121–41; "In forma Dei et forma servi selon saint Hilaire," *Recherches de science religieuse* 48 (1960): 101–18; A. Grillmeier, *Christ in the Christian Tradition* 1: 396f.

[14] Paul Galtier, *Saint Hilaire,* 130.

forma servi. If there is, in fact, no real *evacuatio* in the Incarnation, divine power overcomes the weakness of human nature.

In his later writings Hilary appears to modify this position about the human nature of Jesus.[15] Nevertheless he is clearly in need of a distinction such as that of the *Commentary* from Tura among various types of change. He was on the verge of the same theological discovery, evoked by the same christological text, Phil. 2:6–8. But neither he nor Augustine is able to break away from the language and conceptuality of immutability derived from philosophy and Christian tradition.

AUGUSTINE OF HIPPO

Belief in the Incarnation led Augustine (354–430) to mitigate, at least partially, his well-known insistence on God's absolute immutability. We saw this previously in several Greek fathers from Athanasius on. Christian faith corrected philosophy because of the Arian challenge. Augustine saw this plainly when he wrote the *Confessions.* There he recalls his Photinian view of Jesus and the Apollinarian understanding of Alypius.[16] In referring to his low Christology he wrote, "I had not even an inkling of the meaning of the mystery of the Word made flesh." Christ was subject to change, and the "Word cannot suffer change, as by now I knew in so far as I was able to know it. In fact I had no doubt of it at all." Thus Christ was the perfect man "because in him human nature had reached the highest point of excellence and he had a more perfect share of divine wisdom." But this was a heretical view.

---

[15] See especially *Trac. in Ps. 53:7,* in CSEL 22.140; *De Synodis* 49, in PL 10, 516B–517A.

[16] *Confessions* 7.19.25 in CCL 27: 108–9. Bk. 7.13–27 is one of the most studied sections of this work. See P. Courcelle, *Recherches sur les Confessions de Saint Augustin* (Paris: Boccard, 1960), 157–67; M. Pellegrino, *Les Confessions de Saint Augustin* (Paris: Editions Alsatia, 1960), 162–69; Robert J. O'Connell, *St. Augustine's Confessions* (Cambridge: Harvard, 1969), 75–89; *Augustine's Early Theory of Man* (Cambridge: Harvard, 1968), chap. 1, 43–51; chap. 8; chap. 10; Oliver du Roy, *L'Intelligence de la Foi en la Trinité selon Saint Augustin* (Paris: Etudes Augustiniennes, 1966), 53–106.

From reading the Platonists Augustine had already learned about the existence of the Logos of John's Prologue,[17] but not about its exinanition and Incarnation: "The books also tell us that your only-begotten Son abides for ever in eternity with you; that before all times began, he was; that he is above all time and suffers no change."[18] But they do not teach the most important truth, that which grounds both humility and charity. In reading these books "was I not without charity, which builds its edifice on the firm foundation of humility, that is, on Jesus Christ? But how could I expect that the Platonist books would ever teach me charity?"[19]

In spite of this limitation, "these books served to remind me to return to my own self."[20] They led Augustine to a vision of the divine which he described as the seeing of a transcendent creative light and the hearing of a voice saying "I am the God who Is." This vision of God resulted in an intellectual conversion. Yet importantly, there is something missing in this revelation, which is provided especially by the passage from Paul to which Augustine refers in Book 8. The Word made flesh brings the gift of grace and forgiveness of sin, and the subsequent freedom of the will experienced by Augustine.

Augustine stresses the importance of the Incarnation in three different places in the early Cassiciacum writings. Philosophers would never have found the truth unless God willed in clemency to send the divine intellect down to a human body.[21] "In all three instances where, at Cassiciacum, this union of divinity and humanity is expressly referred to, the stress is placed on the enormous Divine condescension involved."[22] Augustine returns to this theme again and again throughout his corpus. Divine exinanition teaches humility and this is the truth unknown to philosophy.[23]

---

[17] *Conf.* 7.9.13–14, in CCL 27: 101–2.
[18] Ibid.
[19] *Conf.* 7.20.26, in ibid., 110.
[20] *Conf.* 7.10.16, in ibid., 103.
[21] *Contra Acad.* 3.19.42.15–16, in CCL 29, 60–61. Also *De Ordine* 2.9.27, in ibid., 122; 2.5.16, in ibid., 116.
[22] R. O'Connell, *Augustine's Early Theory*, 265.
[23] *Epis.* 118.3.22–4.24, in CSEL 34, 2, 686.

This saving water is not found in Epicureans, Stoics, Manichees, or Platonists. Although discovering the best precepts of custom and discipline, they never find humility. This comes only from Christ who became humble even to death on the cross.[24]

The humility exhibited by the Word in the Incarnation is the cure for pride, the worst of all sins. Only divine humility is true medicine for *superbia*.[25] Augustine expresses this sentiment in language that is surprisingly strong:

> Pride is the source of all diseases, because pride is the source of all sins. . . . Therefore, that the cause of all diseases might be cured, namely pride, the Son of God came down and was made humble. Why are you proud, o man? God was made humble for you. Perhaps you would be ashamed to imitate a humble man; at least imitate a humble God.[26]

It is indeed correct to say that, for Augustine, "it is the humility of Christ which is the most striking feature of the Incarnation."[27] Augustine has grasped precisely that the core of Christian faith is an acceptance of the divine kenosis in Jesus of Nazareth. To get a sense of the impression Phil. 2:6–8 made on Augustine one should consult the Index at the end of *CCL* 50, 699–702. There are two hundred or more citations or allusions to this text in *De Trinitate* alone. Even more impressive is the fact that in Augustine's entire corpus he cites part or all of this passage 422 times, and alludes to it 563 times. Thus he had it in mind nearly a thousand times when he wrote.[28] This passage especially allows

---

[24] "Haec via ab illo est, qui cum esset altus, humilis venit. Quid enim aliud docuit humiliando se, factus oboediens usque ad mortem, mortem autem crucis? Quid aliud docuit nisi hanc humilitatem?" *Enar. in Ps. 31*, 2.18, in CCL 38, 239.

[25] *Sermo* 77.7.11, in ML 38, 488; *Enar. in Ps.18.2.15*, in CCL 38, 112, 26–32; *De Trin.* 8.5.7, in CCL 50, 276, 1–8; *Sermo* 142.2, in ML 38, 778.

[26] *In Jo. Trac.* 25.16, in CCL 36, 256–57.

[27] Gerald Bonner, "Christ, God, and Man in the Thought of St. Augustine," *Angelicum* 61 (1984): 275. See also Otto Schaffner, *Christliche Demut: Des Hl. Augustinus Lehre Von Der Humilitas* (Wurzburg: Augustinus-Verlag, 1959) for an extensive treatment of this idea. It provides no help, however, on the theological issue of divine immutability.

[28] Albert Verwilghen, *Christologie Et Spiritualité Selon Saint Augustine: L'Hymne Aux Philippiens* (Paris: Beauchesne, 1985), 63–64.

Augustine to specify the exact relationship between philosophy and Christian faith. The God of Platonism is only partially identified with the God of Christian faith as Augustine sees it. Strangely, he does not see the limitations of Platonism when he discusses the divine emotions in Scripture. There he is completely content to side with philosophy. The full revelation of the nature of the Christian God as *Deus humilis* comes to him only from belief in the Incarnation.

In any case, we must ask Augustine whether his belief in the humble God led him to revise the philosophical doctrines of divine immutability and impassibility. Did the impact of kenotic Christology cause one of his several rethinkings of his philosophical presuppositions? The answer is clearly no, a conclusion that counters the interpretation given in a recent article by William Mallard.[29]

Mallard sees quite correctly that the Cassiciacum passages and *Confessions* Book 7 imply divine lowering. "The Incarnation of God thus suggests the mutability of God."[30] At the same time, Augustine is fervently committed to divine immutability as we will see frequently in this chapter. Mallard suggests that Augustine reconciled these two attributes by revising his idea of divine perfection so that "the characteristic of tending to lower himself could be considered a perfection of God and therefore reconcilable on an unexpected level with divine immutability."

God's immutability is transformed into the immutable divine *clementia*: "God's mercy in humility is indeed a divine perfection, not inconsistent with his nature as immutable and eternal. For God forever disposes himself graciously and mercifully towards the world."[31] The Neoplatonist philosophers are repudiated: "The immutable perfection of deity is now named as an eternal clemency or mercy, sealed in the self-humbling of Incarnation. Immutability = perfection = perfect goodness = mercy = its actualization in self-abasement."[32] This is exactly what Augustine

---

[29] "The Incarnation in Augustine's Conversion," *Recherches Augustiniennes* 15 (1980): 80–98.

[30] Ibid., 92.

[31] Ibid., 95–96.

[32] Ibid., 98.

should have said, but it is not, however, what he did say. A careful reading of texts shows that Van Bavel is correct on this point; however inconsistent this may be, Augustine believed in the divine kenosis without ever implying an alteration of the divine nature.[33] One finds the strongest evidence to support this interpretation in the Christmas homilies of Augustine.[34] The Incarnation is the assumption of an inferior nature, not the conversion of the superior one.[35] The Word does not change. In beginning to be what he was not, God remains unchanged.[36]

Similar statements abound in Augustine. Incarnation means "not that wisdom was changed, since it is absolutely unchangeable; but that it was his will to make himself known in such humble fashion to men."[37] In regard to Phil. 2:6–7 he writes: "When he accepted the form of a servant, he accepted time. Did he change therefore? Was he lessened? Was he exiled? Did he fall into defect? No . . . He was lowered by accepting an inferior, not by degenerating from equality."[38] Again, "[the Word] was made visible not through a change in Its own nature, but by Its being attired in the clothing of our nature. . . . In this way, the soul finds Him whom it forsook in pride, outwardly humble, and will imitate his visible humility."[39] Several other texts might be cited in defense of this position, but unnecessarily. Augustine did not see the full philosophical implications of Christian belief in the Incarnation, because he was totally committed to divine immutability as a philosophical axiom.

---

[33] T. J. Van Bavel, *Recherches sur la Christologie de Saint Augustine: l'humain et le divin dans le Christ d'apres saint Augustin* (Fribourg: Editions Universitaires, 1954), 11.

[34] ML 38, 995f. English in S. M. S. Muldowney, *Sermons on the liturgical season* FC (New York: Fathers of the Church, Inc.: 1959), v.38: 3–48.

[35] *Serm.* 186.2.2–3.3 in ML 38, 1000: "Ac per hoc qui erat Dei Filius, factus est hominis filius, assumptione inferioris, non conversione potioris; accipiendo quod non erat, non amittendo quod erat."

[36] "Verbum autem domini manet in aeternum, et incommutabiliter manet," in ibid., 1002; also 1003.

[37] *De fide et Symbol.* 9. 18.

[38] "Demutatus est ergo? deminutus est? exilior redditus? in defectum lapsus? Absit. Exinaninisse se dictus est accipiendo inferiorem, non degenerando ab aequali." *Enar. in Ps. 74:5* in CCL 39, 1028.

[39] *De libero arbitrio* 3.10.30 in CCL 29, 293.

The Divine Immutability

Even a surface reading shows that Augustine is "intransigent in his contention that God is absolutely immutable."[40] To a great extent this intransigence is due to the influence of the Neo-Platonic understanding of God.[41] Indeed for Augustine himself, immutability may have been God's most important attribute, "the basis on which other attributes rest, the root from which they spring."[42] Many passages in Augustine's works suggest this.[43] Even if such is not the case, however, we are certainly dealing with a central affirmation. It is one that cannot be revised without calling into question the theological adequacy of his entire conception of God. His christological insights do exactly this.

Augustine's reasons for insisting on divine immutability are many. Absolute immutability grounds the immutability of truth;[44] it also distinguishes God from all creatures, including the soul and angels that are spiritual like God;[45] it is essential to God's

---

[40] Bernard J. Cooke, "The Mutability-Immutability Principle in St. Augustine's Metaphysics," *Modern Schoolman* 24 (November, 1946): 43.

[41] For a complete treatment of Augustine's philosophical milieu, as well as his relation to patristic theology generally, see R. Holte, *Beatitude et sagesse: saint Augustin et la probleme de la fin de l'homme dans la philosophie ancienne* (Paris: Etudes Augustiniennes, 1962).

[42] Cooke, "Mutability-Immutability," 42. This is not the view of all other scholars, as Cooke indicates. Some think divine simplicity lies at the root of Augustine's conception of God. Another possibility is that of divine spirituality. There is a good possibility that none of God's attributes is in fact the root of all the others, but that all imply each other. Augustine sometimes emphasizes one, and sometimes another.

[43] For immutability texts in Augustine see Martin Grabmann, *Die Grundgedanken des heiligen Augustinus über Seele und Gott* (Darmstadt: Wissenschaftliche Buchgesellschaft, 1967); M. Schmaus, *Die psychologische Trinitätslehre des heiligen Augustinus* (Munster: Aschendorff, 1967), 90f.; W. P. Tolley, *The Idea of God in the Philosophy of St. Augustine* (New York: Richard R. Smith, 1930).

[44] *De doctrina Christiana* 1.8.8, in CCL 32, 11; *Conf.* 12.25.34–35, in CCL 27, 234–36; *De libero arbitrio* 2. chap. 3ff, in CCL 29, 239f. See J. Barion, *Plotin und Augustinus: Untersuchungen zum Göttesproblem* (Berlin: Junker & Dunnhaupt, 1935), 59f.

[45] *De Civ.* 4.31, in CCL 47, 126; 8.5, in ibid. 222 states that to ascribe mutability that the soul has to the divine nature is *nefas*. In 8.6, in ibid. 223 he argues divine simplicity and immutability simultaneously. Also 11.10, in CCL 48, 330.

perfection;[46] and God is immutable because of being eternally beyond time.[47]

Because God cannot change, God is impassible. Contrary to some biblical passages, God cannot have feelings. The Bible and the Christian tradition have characteristically attributed feelings to God, even "unworthy" feelings such as wrath, jealousy, and regret for a former decision. These attributions became acutely problematic for Augustine, as they were for Christian writers before him.[48] Tertullian's main opponent here was Marcion, who denied the goodness of the God of Judaism outright. Divine wrath, jealousy, and the arbitrary ability to change mind and will were characteristics unworthy of the Father of Jesus. For Augustine, the Manichees raised this question in somewhat the same fashion. In this religion, "the stern Jehovah of the Jews was rejected as a malevolent demon."[49] Augustine must show that God does not literally have unworthy feelings because God does not change. He does have to defend the truth of the Hebrew Scriptures, however, against Manichean criticism. Augustine also rejects a literal understanding of the more "worthy" divine emotions such as God's love and mercy. No feeling whatsoever is appropriate to the divine immutable essence. God is impassible because God is immutable.

---

[46] *Conf.* 7.17.23, in CCL 27, 107; 13.16.19, in ibid., 252; *De Trin.* 5.2.3, in CCL 50, 208; *De Civ.* 12. 1–2, in CCL 48, 355–57.

[47] *De Civ.* 7.22, in CCL 47, 203. This is especially clear in those passages where Augustine defends God's eternal immutable foreknowledge and will, such as *De Civ.* 5.9, in CCL 47, 136–140; *Enchiridion* 95–106, in CCL 46, 99–107; *De Div.* 11.21, in CCL 48, 339; 12.17, in ibid., 373. See Wilma Gundersdorf Von Jess, "Divine Eternity in the Doctrine of St. Augustine," *Augustinian Studies* 6 (1975): 75–96. In the second section of her dissertation she argues convincingly that all God's attributes are melded or blended into one another by Augustine. *The Divine Attributes in the Thought of St. Augustine* (Ph.D. diss.: Boston College, 1971), 98–99.

[48] See Cornelius Meyer, ed. "Affectus" in *Augustinus-Lexicon* (Basel/Stüttgart: Schwabe, 1986) v. 1, c. 166–80.

[49] Peter Brown, *Augustine of Hippo: A Biography* (Berkeley and Los Angeles: University of California, 1969) 50. For an excellent discussion of Augustine's method of biblical interpretation, see H. I. Marrou, *St. Augustin et la fin de la culture antique* (Paris: E. de Boccard, 1958): 469–503.

God's Anger

Augustine's favorite explanation for God's anger as portrayed in
Scripture is that it is the divine punishment for sin, but has no
perturbatio accompanying it. God judges and condemns the sinner while feeling nothing: "We must take care, however, to understand that the anger of God is free from any turbulent
emotion; for His anger is an expression for His just method of
taking vengeance; as the law might be said to be angry when its
ministers are moved to punish by its sanctions."[50]

God's anger is only "just retribution," but not "perturbation
of the mind."[51] Divine anger is not like ours, because ours is
irrational.[52] The power that God has to punish sinners is called
anger only "metaphorically from custom."[53] It is "transferred by
analogy from human emotions,"[54] and it applies to "the effect of
His vengeance, not to the disturbing mental affection."[55] The
fact that God is said to be angry is "an abuse of the word, or a
peculiarity of idiom."[56] Because God knows from all eternity
those upon whom punishment will fall, he need not respond
temporally and mutably to their sins as they are committed. His
anger is only a "just and fixed" condemnation of sinners.[57] "The
anger of God is not a disturbing emotion of His mind, but a
judgment by which punishment is inflicted upon sin. . . . His
decision is as inflexible as His prescience is certain."[58]

In one place Augustine suggests that every judgment of
God can be called divine *ira*. Sometimes God judges to perfect,
and sometimes to condemn. Here the divine anger is reduced to
judgment completely, since even the judgment of the saint is

---

[50] *Enar. in Ps.82:12,* in CCL 39, 1144. I am indebted in this treatment to the
short article by J.-C. Fredouille, "Sur la colere divine: Jamblique et Augustin," in
Recherches Augustiniennes 5 (1968), 7–13. Fredouille lists approximately twenty
texts of Augustine on divine anger (8–9).
[51] *De Trin.* 13.16, in CCL 50a, 411.
[52] *Quest. in Hept.* 2.10, in CCL 33, 72; *De patientia* 1.1, in PL 40, c. 611.
[53] *Enar. in Ps.* 105.32, in CCL 40, 1565.
[54] *Enchir.* 10.33, in CCL 46, 68.
[55] *De Civ.* 9.5, in CCL 47, 254; *Enchir.* 29.112, in CCL 46, 109.
[56] *Contra Faust.* 22.18, in CSEL 25, 1, 607.
[57] *Epist.* 190.10, in CSEL 57, 145.
[58] *De Civ.* 15.25, in CCL 48, 493.

wrathful.[59] And this is not God's temporal response in either case, but is eternally willed. Divine anger is nothing more than the eternal condemnation of the sinner, or perfecting of the saint.

Augustine occasionally gives other explanations for God's wrath. He sometimes thinks of it as a holy anger which is felt, not by God, but by a holy soul when it sees the divine law broken by a sinner. He also suggests that God's anger might be an obscuring of the mind of the sinner. In both cases divine anger does not apply to God at all.[60] Augustine gives this psychological explanation most persuasively in his last text on the subject:[61]

> When God is said to change His will, as when, e.g., He becomes angry with those to whom He was gentle, it is rather they than He who are changed, and they find Him changed in so far as their experience of suffering at His hand is new, as the sun is changed to injured eyes, and becomes as it were fierce from being mild, and hurtful from being delightful, though in itself it remains the same as it was.[62]

Uncharacteristic of Augustine's discussions of divine anger is yet another suggestion that shows his pessimism at that point about life. God's anger is another word for human existence. "For God's anger is this mortal life, in which man is made like to vanity, and his days pass as a shadow."[63] The wrath of God is the punishment of death for Adam's sin, as well as all the evils of life which precede death, evils which will be done away with in the afterlife. Our present life is "full of temptation, cares, bodily sorrows, and indigences. We are mutable and feeble even when we are healthy, because we are not yet fully healthy."[64] Augustine's usual

---

[59] *Enar. in Ps. 58 serm. 2.6,* in CCL 39, 750.

[60] *Enar. in Ps. 2,4,* in CCL 38, 4.

[61] According to Fredouille, "Sur la colere," 10.

[62] *De Civ.* 22.2, in CCL 48, 807. Also *De Trin.* 5.16.17, in CCL 50, 227.

[63] *De Civ.* 21.24, in CCL 48, 790–91.

[64] *Enar. in Ps.37.5* in CCL 38, 384–85. Pinomaa plausibly suggests but does not establish a dichotomy between Augustine the theoretician and Augustine the religious man regarding the divine anger. "Als religiöser Mensch hat er dagegen das Gericht Gottes also eine erschütternde Wirklichkeit empfunde, wovon seine Schriften genügend Zeugnis ablegen." L. Pinomaa, "Der Zorn Gottes. Eine dogmengeschichtliche Übersicht," *Zeitschrift für systematische Theologie* 17 (1940):

explanation for God's anger, however, is that it is an idiomatic, metaphorical, and possibly improper term for the punishment of sinners which God eternally foreknows and immutably wills.

God's Repentance

The Scriptural passages that were especially problematic for Augustine are the same as those we have seen before. Some state that God repents for a former decision. The author of Gen. 6:7 visualizes the creator of the world as regretting the creation of the sinful human race: "I repent that I made man." First Sam. 15:11 and 15:35 state that God repents for having set up Saul to be king. As a result God rejects Saul and chooses David. A third case is that of the Ninevites. "When God saw what they did, how they turned from their evil ways, God changed his mind about the calamity that he had said he would bring upon them; and he did not do it."[65] If literally interpreted, these passages contradict divine immutability and impassibility, as well as foreknowledge. They also might suggest that God can make mistakes. Sorrow for a former action may indicate lack of knowledge about some outcome, and therefore an incorrect or unwise choice. A study of these texts in Hebrew obviates most of these difficulties, but Augustine knew no Hebrew and little Greek.

Tertullian offered a good solution to this problem by arguing from the Greek term *metanoia*. Only a simple change of prior purpose or change of mind is involved, which does not necessarily imply confession of sin, or making a mistake. Tertullian was willing to admit that God could undergo this change of mind, seeing it as a divine prerogative. But Augustine deals with the text in the light of his belief in absolute immutability, as well as the Latin phrase *poenitet me*, and its explicit reference to sorrow for a prior decision. Neither sorrow nor error can be in God.[66] It

603. As a religious person, Augustine experienced his "Dasein unter dem Zorn Gottes." 613.

[65] Jon. 3:10; also Amos 7:3 and 6; Jer.18:8; 1 Chron. 21:15a; Ps. 106:45.

[66] "Non enim dolorem paenitentiae patitur Deus, aut in aliquo fallitur, ut velit corrigere in quo erravit." *Enar. in Ps. 131.18*, in CCL 40, 1920.

is in regard to this problem that Augustine gives his most radical interpretation of biblical passibility or mutability texts. Passages such as these, he says, do not properly express God's nature. Those passages that do properly express it are found only rarely in the divine Scriptures![67]

Repentance is simply impossible for God, since complete foreknowledge and regret for a decision cannot coexist. Therefore we deny penitence, he says.[68] That something could be temporally added to God's knowledge is *absurdissimum atque falsissimum.* Therefore, in spite of what Scriptures say, God does not repent. Augustine writes later in this passage that God repents in some ineffable manner, and this is clearly a weakening of the *negamus* that precedes it.[69]

Augustine also offers solutions that are less radical. In one of his best discussions of divine repentance, he explains how the scriptural references to God's emotions are improper expressions, just like those that refer to God's feet, face, hands, and eyes. Such expressions are used because of custom, and because of the poverty of human expression. The inspired authors knew full well that God did not literally have emotions, or a body. God's hand is the power of operation; feet signify the power of governing and caring for all things; ears and eyes refer to the power of perception and knowledge; God's face is the power by which the divine is manifested in the world. By the same reasoning, divine repentance is the divine providence by which the world is calmly administrated by God. Specifically, God's repentance refers to those things which providentially pass out of existence contrary to our wishes.[70]

In another place Augustine gives the same type of solution, referring divine repentance to our perception of a specific type of providence. "The repentance of God refers to things ruled by

---

[67] "Raro ponit scriptura divina." *De Trin.* 1.1.2, in CCL 50, 29. One passage that does contain a proper expression is Ex. 3:14, which he, with the tradition beginning with Philo, believes refers to God's metaphysical essence.

[68] "Negamus poenitentiam." *De div. quest. ad Simpl.* 2.2.2, in CCL 44, 76.

[69] 2.2.2, in ibid., 77. Further weakening is evident in 2.2.5, ibid., 80–81.

[70] "Ea quae incipiunt esse neque perseverant, quantum perseveratura sperata sunt, quasi per penitentiam dei dicuntur." *De div. quaest.* 52, in CCL 48A, 83.

his power which change unexpectedly for us."[71] This explanation is the same as his final statement about God's anger, that it is only something we perceive, and not something that is objectively present in God.

All of Augustine's interpretations of the repentance passages suggest either outright denial, or that divine repentance for decisions is only a subjective perception of ours, a perception of a providence that is eternally unchanging. In discussing Jon. 3:10, he says that God is not uncertain about the repentance of the Ninevites, but only seems so.[72] Regarding Gen. 6:7, he reaffirms the doctrine that God does not change, and the divine judgment only appears to change, that is, to us.[73] God exchanged David for Saul, thereby changing his works, but changing them "through his own immutable will."[74] In effect, Augustine's explanation for these passages is that God does not repent at all because God cannot, and the divine statutes only change from our viewpoint.[75]

Jealousy

A third divine emotion that was problematic for Augustine was jealousy.[76] The basis for this divine quality comes from passages such as Exodus 20:5; 34:15; Deut. 4:24 and 2 Cor. 11:2. These texts also caused problems for earlier Christian writers in debates with the Marcionites. Here as in the case of repentance, Augustine's choice is clear. He must either deny that God can become jealous, or, less radically, interpret God's jealousy as some quality that does not contradict immutability and

---

[71] *Contra advers. Legis et Prophet.* 1.20.40, in PL 42, 627. This is a comment on a verse from Ps. 109: "Juravit dominus, et non poenitebit eum. Tu es sacerdos."

[72] "Aliter quidem videtur hominibus, et aliter visum est Deo." *Enar. in Ps. 50.11*, in CCL 38, 607.

[73] *Sermo* 22.6, in CCL 41, 296.

[74] *Enar. in Ps. 131.18*, in CCL 40, 1920. In support of this interpretation he cites Ps. 109 (110):4. He cites this verse in the same context in *Contra advers. Legis et Prophet.* 1.20.40, in PL 42, 627.

[75] *De Civ.* 14.11, in CCL 48, 431.

[76] See Pierre Adnes, "Jealousie de Dieu," *Dictionnaire de Spiritualité* 8 (Paris: Beauchesne, 1974), 79–93.

impassibility. He generally follows the latter course, describing God's jealousy as eternal unchanging providence or justice as applied to certain specific situations.

We cannot deny God's jealousy, he writes, because it is found in the Scriptures. But we must uphold it in some way that is far removed from the case of jealousy because of unchastity. We must derive another understanding in God's case. Since the anger of God is not a mental disturbance but a power to punish, his jealousy is not the excruciating emotion that accompanies marital jealousy, but tranquil and sincere justice and providence.[77]

At times Augustine comes closer to a literal understanding of God's jealousy than he does for any other unworthy emotion, and seems to want to uphold it properly as an emotion. After one purges the feeling of any unworthy quality, it must necessarily be applied to God. God is jealous "as when diligence is manifested in guarding conjugal chastity, in which sense it is profitable for us not only unhesitatingly to admit but thankfully to assert, that God is jealous of his people when He calls them His wife."[78] In another anti-Manichean text, Augustine affirms his principle that "nothing is able to be said that is worthy of God."[79] A prime example of this is the statement that the Word of God came down from heaven, even though it cannot move from place to place, because it is present everywhere. But if we take away error and sorrow from our notion of jealousy, nothing remains except the will to guard chastity and to condemn conjugal corruption. What better word is there to express the will of God to keep us from love of corrupt things, his will to love our chastity, and to punish our unchastity? For a God "who is not jealous does not love."[80] The consuming fire that is combined with jealousy in Deut. 4:24 is God's love for us, and his jealousy is part of that love.

---

[77] *Contra Adim. Man. Discipl.* 11, in CSEL 25, 136. Also *Contra Advers. Legis et Prophet.* 1.20.40, in PL 42, 627. Here the *providentia* is defined precisely to match the biblical idea of God's jealousy. It is "providentia quae non sinit eos quos subditos habet impune amare quod prohibet."

[78] *Contra Faust.* 22.18, in CSEL 25, 607.

[79] *Contra Adim. Man. Discipl.* 13, in CSEL 25, 144.

[80] Ibid., 146.

Earlier in this same work, after stating the principle that the Scriptures are incapable of expressing divine things properly, Augustine says that God's jealousy is the power and discipline that prevent the soul from fornicating with impunity. God prevents the spiritual fornication that turns toward temporal things and away from the divine.[81] This preventive aspect of divine providence is also said to keep the soul from being corrupted by following false gods.[82] Although he defends God's jealousy and seems to sense its propriety even as a divine emotion, ultimately Augustine reduces it, like God's anger, to some aspect of eternal providence or justice.

Within the confines of Augustine's theology, it is difficult if not impossible to defend the literal reality of divine emotions such as regret, anger, or jealousy. Yet the fact that God is portrayed as emotional was important, at least for Tertullian before him. Augustine apparently perceived this at least in the case of jealousy. Is there no sense in which God can be said to be surprised at the depths of human sinfulness? Is it not religiously significant that God can react negatively to our deeds? Did God never really hear the prayers of the Ninevites and respond temporally to their penitence by changing God's will? Is there no possible divine response to the world which can legitimately be called God's anger? Is there no jealousy that is Scripturally and religiously appropriate to the divine? In this last case Augustine himself suggests that there is, although by the philosophical ideas to which he is committed, there cannot be. Augustine's theology does not allow for the systematic expression of these important religious insights into the divine character.

God's Love and Mercy

At the end of his long and well-known discussion of time in Book 11 of the *Confessions*, Augustine writes:

---

[81] Ibid., 7. 129. A discussion of 2 Cor. 11:2.
[82] *De div. quaest.* 52, in CCL 44A, 83.

Therefore, just as in the beginning you have known heaven and earth without change in your knowledge so too "in the beginning you made heaven and earth" without any difference in your activity. Whosoever understands this, let him confess it to you, and whosoever does not understand it, let him confess it to you.[83]

In another passage in the *Confessions* he distinguishes four types of priority which might apply to that of God over creation, then states that the type that God has is rarely seen and difficult to conceive.[84] While he does give a type of solution to the question of God's priority,[85] the deeper problem that he must resolve is how to describe the relation between God and his creatures without making God mutable and passible. Does God's relationship to creatures begin to be for God as well as for creatures? Is God continuously affected by it? What does it mean to say that God loves and forgives, as well as creates in time?

De Trinitate 5.16.17 attempts to answer these questions systematically.[86] In some sense, Augustine says, God became the Lord of creation, and the Lord of Israel. He gives various examples of the occurrence of new relations, such as that of a carpenter to a wooden chest that he makes. But this does not apply to God. So far as God is concerned, there can only be relations which cause change on the side of his effects, and not in the divine nature. The first real example Augustine gives for the God-world relation is that of friendship. He cannot press this for an obvious reason. Friendship necessitates reciprocity.

The second example is that of money, which can be either a price or a pledge, without undergoing any change because of its relationship to one or the other, or both simultaneously. The relation between God and creatures can begin to be in time, although nothing happens to the substance of God. In the same manner, money can begin to be a price or pledge without itself becoming anything different. "O Lord," it is said, "you are our refuge." God

---

[83] *Conf.* 11.31.41, in CCL 27, 216.
[84] *Conf.* 12.29.40, in ibid., 239.
[85] See *De Civ.* 4–6, in CCL 48, 323–26.
[86] *De Trin.* 5.16.17, in CCL 50, 226f.

becomes our refuge only so far as we are concerned, but not so far as God is concerned. Did something happen in God's nature that was not happening before we took refuge? No. There is some change in us, but none in God.

God begins to be our Father when we are regenerated by divine grace. But there is a change only in us, not in God. Augustine states the theological principle that applies to all cases of the divine in its relation to creatures:

> Therefore, anything that begins to be said of Him in time, which had not been attributed to Him previously, is evidently spoken of relatively, but such expressions are not used according to an accident of God, as though something new had taken place in Him, but plainly according to an accident of that creature with whom God, according to our manner of speaking, entered a relationship.[87]

Therefore God cannot begin to love someone. When we find God, we only say that God begins to love us, but this is incorrect if believed literally. "He loved and predestined all his saints before the constitution of the world." God does not begin to love us without loving us eternally. "So, too, when we speak of Him as being . . . gentle towards the good; it is they who are changed, not He; just as light is painful to weak eyes and pleasing to strong eyes, namely, by their change, not its own." In another passage, Augustine collapses the relation of love between God and creatures into God's giving of being to creatures in general.[88] The solution to the problem of how an immutable creator can create a mutable world, then, "solves" the problem of God's love as well.

How does God love us, he asks? So that God might use and enjoy us? If God enjoys us, God needs us, and no sane person would say this. God is our every good, or our every good comes from God. Therefore, God does not enjoy us because God does not need us. Yet God does use us. For if God does neither, Augustine writes, I cannot discover how God loves us! He then

---

[87] Ibid., 227.
[88] *De doctrina Christiana* 1.31.34, in CCL 32, 26.

hastens to add that God cannot use us in the way that we use created things. His use of us is connected to divine goodness. It can only mean that "because he is good, we are, and in so far as we are, we are good." Instead of God enjoying us, or making use of us in some way that these words imply, God causes us to exist, and that is what it means to say that God loves us.

Mercy

Since God cannot truly feel love for his creatures, neither can he feel mercy. Human mercy is accompanied by a feeling of misery of heart, *miser-icordia*, which God cannot have. Human misery of heart accompanies the feelings of mercy or compassion, because by means of human compassion, one shares the misery of the one pitied.[89] It is impossible for the divine essence to be disturbed by such an emotion, worthy as it is:

> With regard to pity, if you take away the compassion which involved a sharing of misery with him whom you pity, so that there remains the peaceful goodness of helping and freeing from misery, some kind of knowledge of the divine pity is suggested.[90]

This text is important in that it suggests that God does feel something, albeit purged of the human emotion of "sharing of misery." God feels the peaceful goodness of helping and freeing from misery, and this gives some meaning to the divine pity. Yet the most obvious interpretation of this feeling is that it is no feeling at all, and that divine mercy is reduced to God's giving of being to those who are saved. God's peaceful goodness is only

---

[89] *Contra Adimant. Man. Discipl.* 11 in CSEL 25, 137; *De div. quaest.* 2.2.3, in CCL 44, 79; *Contra Advers. Legis et Prophet.* 1.20.40 in PL 42, 627. In *De Civ.* 9.5, in CCL 47, 254: "What is mercy but a certain feeling of compassion in our hearts, evoked by the misery of another and compelling us to offer all possible aid?" See Theodore Koehler, "Misericorde," in *Dictionnaire de Spiritualité* 10 (Paris: Beauchesne, 1979), 1322–23. He rightly stresses the importance of this attribute for Augustine. Nevertheless Augustine denies that God can truly have such a feeling of compassion "evoked by the misery of another" lest God become passible and mutable.

[90] *De div. quaest.* 2.2.3, in CCL 44, 79.

the eternally foreknown and predestined giving of grace to the saints. The ability to help and to free creatures from misery can be only God's eternal predestination of some souls before the constitution of the world, which is equivalent to the giving of their existence in grace.[91] In the final analysis it is emotionless, although Augustine perhaps wished that it were otherwise. God's mercy is nontemporal so far as God is concerned.

He describes the divine emotions in summary fashion in the following way:

> God's repentance is not because of error; his anger has no ardor of a perturbed mind; his mercy does not have the compassionate misery suggested by the Latin term; the jealousy of God has no spite of mind. But the repentance of God refers to things ruled by his power which change unexpectedly for us; the anger of God is the punishment of sin; the mercy of God is the goodness of helping; the jealousy of God is providence, which does not allow those which it has subdued to love with impunity what it prohibits.[92]

There is indeed some difference between a denial that God can regret decisions, and the suggestion that an unexpected and perceptible change in human affairs ruled by providence appears to be a divine change of will to us, although such is not really the case. Also there is a difference between seeing God's jealousy as justice and providence in general, or more specifically as providential punishment for improper human loving. There is a difference between an outright denial that God can be angry and the reduction of divine anger to our perception, or to punishment for sin. Finally, God can validly be said to love us and to have mercy on us, because God creates and predestines us for salvation. Augustine defends the divine emotions by placing them in our perception, or by reducing them to impassible divine qualities of providence, justice, punishment for sin, or God's eternal action toward us which does not involve change. God seems to feel

---

[91] *Contra Advers. Legis et Prophet.* 1.20.40, in PL 42, 627. See also *De div. quaest.* 1.2.7, in CCL 44, 31–32 where God's mercy precedes faith and is not a response at all. Also *Retract.* 1.24, in PL 32, 626.

[92] *Contra Advers. Legis et Prophet.* 1.20.40 in PL 42, 627.

anger, jealousy, and regret, and even love and the calm goodness which comes from helping others. But God, in fact, feels nothing.

In a certain sense, Augustine standardizes the discussion of the question of divine immutability and impassibility in Western Christianity. From now on it will be situated, as will nearly all theological questions, within the framework that he provides. That framework should have included more of an emphasis on the divine humility. Augustine is important to this study because, although God is immutable and impassible for him, the Incarnate Word is *Deus humilis*. This points the way to another view, one that could have taken divine mutability and passibility seriously on the philosophical level. Obviously, Augustine did not develop this view. It has had to wait until modern times.

6

THE GREAT COMPANION
*Hegel, Whitehead, and
Divine Suffering*

The question of divine suffering and change in the Incarnation did not disappear after Augustine. Especially because of the Alexandrian emphasis on the personal unity of the Incarnate Logos and divine personal identity, various interpretations of the Incarnation were possible. These gave rise to monophysitism, monotheletism, and the theopaschite controversies. And even though Scholasticism eventually wrestled with the logical questions of unity of person and distinction of natures, the issue appeared again in the theological insistence of Martin Luther (1483–1546) that God truly suffered in Jesus.

John the Scot (born c. 810) is the only Christian thinker of importance in the long period between Augustine and Anselm. In the *Peri physeon*, he reflects on the divine love. Love involves acting and being acted upon and both imply change. Yet the deity, being perfect, is immutable. Since neither action nor passion can apply literally to God, it follows that God "does not move and is not moved, does not love and is not loved." At this point, John pauses:

> This last conclusion demands considerable thought, for I believe
> that the authority of the whole sacred Scripture and of the holy

fathers appears to oppose it. As you know, sacred Scripture often explicitly states that God acts and is acted upon, loves and is loved, cherishes and is cherished, sees and is seen, moves and is moved, and so on.[1]

If "God does not love, is not loved, does not move, is not moved . . . you see with how many formidable shafts of sacred Scripture I shall be overwhelmed. The Scriptural passages seem to shout on all sides and to declare this view is false."[2] Eventually John appeals to Pseudo-Dionysius. In condescension to our weakness, Scripture uses words or names that are not literal, but only metaphorical.[3] Thus in the end, God is only said to love because he is the cause of love,[4] and he is "said to be loved by all things that are from Him, not because He is acted upon by them in any way (for He alone is incapable of being acted upon), but because they all long for him."[5]

John repeats a familiar answer to this question. Although the God of Christian faith is a creator and companion, a redeemer and savior, the divine is by nature incapable of change, emotion, or suffering of any kind because these imply imperfection. In spite of belief in the creation of the world, the election and redemption of Israel, and the Incarnation of the Logos in Jesus of Nazareth, Christian authors from the Apologists to Augustine teach with nearly one voice that God is immutable and impassible.

Like John the Scot, Anselm (1033–1109) certainly saw the problem but could not resolve it.[6] To believe in the Incarnation of the Word of God who, while remaining divine, became human, and yet to hold to divine immutability and impassibility in an absolute way, is contradictory. Thomas Aquinas (1224–1274) applies the concept of a relation that is real and involves change on the part of human nature, but is only a relation of reason on God's part. Hence the being of God remains unaffected by

---

[1] Myra L. Uhlfelder, *Peri physeon* (Indianapolis: Bobbs-Merrill, 1976), p. 80.

[2] Ibid., p. 85. See Henry Bett, *Joannes Scotus Erigena* (New York: Russell, 1964), p. 27, for a concise summary of John on this point.

[3] *Peri physeon,* p. 86.

[4] Ibid., p. 99–100.

[5] Ibid.

[6] See his *Proslogion* 8 and *Cur Deus Homo* 1.8.

becoming human. Anselm and Thomas, as well as all others who discussed divine immutability and impassibility before modern times, with few exceptions, only repeated, expanded, or refined positions held by Augustine.

The Christian tradition has always needed a different philosophical point of departure to express its radical religious intuition, one which absorbs in an intellectual way the personal reality of the God of Scripture, and specifically the myth/symbol of divine descent. If one appreciates the greatness of the minds of Greek philosophers, it is no wonder that their view of God remained fundamentally unchallenged by Christian theologians in the West through the Middle Ages up to and including the Reformation. It is also easy to understand how the distancing of God from the cosmos and from human affairs in the theological tradition prepared the way for the Enlightenment, the rise of modern science, deism, secularism, and modern atheism.

The two strands of European philosophy, the idealistic and the empirical, led to the construction of two modern systems of thought, quite different from one another, both attempting to overcome this distancing. These two strands reached their high points in the metaphysics of Georg Wilhelm Friedrich Hegel (1770–1831) and Alfred North Whitehead (1861–1947). Both created systems which are at least implicitly religious. They elucidate the basic Christian intuition concerning incarnation, that the reality of God is perfection in change. In so doing, they overcame the main limitation of Greek philosophy.

Enlightenment philosophers had located the divine even further from creation and from human experience than the classical tradition, and although both Hegel and Whitehead have their precedents, they present, each in his own way, uniquely original interpretations of the message of Christianity that the divine has lowered itself to the created level.

HEGEL

It is to the genius of Hegel that we can attribute the discovery in modern times of the significance of the Incarnation. His is the first metaphysical attempt to recover the symbol of John 1:14 in terms of the divine nearness and self-completion. In a way he is simply repeating what Athanasius and other patristic writers believed about the divinisation of humanity, but with a metaphysics of change which they lacked.

For Hegel the basic content of revealed religion, that is, Christianity, was the Incarnation, the *Menschwerdung*. In order to make this more explicit, I will refer to Jesus although Hegel does not do so. The Incarnation is not to be conceived as the occasional visitation of a divine being in the human form of the man Jesus which is so much a part of the Christian community, haunted as it is by Greco-Roman mythology. It is a true and permanent self-revelation of Spirit which knows itself through its externalization. In this very externalization or *Menschwerdung*, Spirit becomes self-conscious in Jesus: "Spirit is known as self-consciousness and to this self-consciousness it is immediately revealed, for Spirit is this self-consciousness itself. The divine nature is the same as the human, and it is this unity that is beheld."[7]

Although the Incarnation is pictured as a descent, it is in reality the attainment of Spirit's highest essence, which is to become the concrete human individual. "Spirit, in the immediacy of self-consciousness, is *this individual* self-consciousness, and so is an antithesis to the universal self-consciousness."[8] One need only compare this to Plato and Plotinus to notice how radically Hegel departs from their theology. They insist that the divine stay where it is, keeping its own attributes, and that we ascend to it by means of our own souls or spirits which are radically connected to but distinct from it. In Hegel's view, this static conception is overcome, along with the distinction between divine and human spirit. In Jesus, divine universal self-consciousness becomes the human individual self-consciousness of this man.

Incarnation does not cease with the single instance of Jesus however:

---

[7] A. V. Miller, trans., *The Phenomenology of Spirit* (Oxford: Clarendon Press, 1977), 460. I use this translation throughout with attention to the German in texts that I quote. Page numbers are from this translation.

[8] Ibid., 461.

> This individual man, then, which absolute Being has revealed itself
> to be, accomplishes in himself as an individual the movement of
> sensuous Being. He is the *immediately* present God; consequently,
> his "being" passes over into "having been."[9]

The *Menschwerdung* of a single individual becomes past when
Jesus passes out of existence: "Consciousness, for which God is
thus sensuously present, ceases to see and hear Him; it has seen
and heard Him; and it is because it only *has* seen and heard Him
that it first becomes itself spiritual consciousness."[10]

The moment of single incarnation must pass into objectivity
in order to allow the community to grasp itself as Spirit incarnate.
The remoteness of the single incarnation of Jesus in time and
space raises it into the "realm of picture thinking" and it is through
picture thinking that the community "becomes aware of itself."[11]
The very past-ness of the Incarnation as recalled to the community by its liturgy enables that community to realize its true nature. To put it negatively, unless Jesus goes away and recedes into
living memory, the fullness of the presence of Spirit cannot occur
in the community. "I must go to my Father." This new communal
awareness springs from the new presence of the Paraclete.

Picturing the Incarnation as a past event makes it appear to be
external, however. Spirit must move away from mere external representation and otherness to more complete self-consciousness,
that is, to the knowledge that each self-consciousness is an incarnation of Spirit. Depending upon whether members of the community find the representations of religion satisfactory, they have
either an unhappy or a believing consciousness. The first results in
the Spirit's self-conscious dissatisfaction with its own content. It
sees picturing as picturing and as external to itself. In other words
Christian memory is only of past irrelevant images that do not bear
on the present. In fact, for many modern Christians, religious

---

[9] Ibid., 462.

[10] Ibid.

[11] Ibid., 464. "Picture-thinking" is Miller's translation of *Vorstellung*, which
means more exactly "representation." This is the translation favored by James
Yerkes. See his careful discussion in *The Christology of Hegel* (Albany: SUNY Press,
1983), 71–89.

picturing is perceived as an illegitimate intrusion upon their integrity as modern persons, driving them away from religion.

Believing consciousness accepts in faith an objective religious content which is external. Such is the faith of fundamentalists who accept external pictures at the expense of internal integrity. It "simply flees from reality and consequently is without the certainty of self-consciousness." In both cases, that of ex-believer or believer, Spirit has not yet grasped its true identity because it has a self-consciousness which is incomplete.

The representations of the religious community are continually problematic according to the *Phenomenology.* Believers degrade religious content "into a historical pictorial idea" which becomes "an heirloom handed down by tradition."[12] In order to transcend the pictorial way of thinking, Spirit must attain a universality of self-consciousness precisely in the individuals within a community: "The movement of the community as self-consciousness that has distinguished itself from its picture-thought is to make explicit what has been implicitly established. The dead divine Man or human God is *in himself* the universal consciousness."[13] The death of the Mediator which is simultaneously the death of the symbol of individual and unique incarnation signifies for Hegel the supersession of incarnation as an individual phenomenon by an incarnation that is universal. Such a supersession involves the death of the symbol of Jesus as Incarnate Lord.

> The death of this picture-thought contains, therefore, at the same time the death of the *abstraction of the divine Being* which is not posited as Self. That death is the painful feeling of the Unhappy Consciousness that *God Himself is dead.* This hard saying is the expression of the innermost simple self-knowledge, the return of consciousness into the depths of the night in which "I" = "I."[14]

---

[12] Miller, *Phenomenology,* 466.
[13] Ibid., 473.
[14] Ibid., 476.

Although one cannot help but think of Feuerbach and Nietzsche here, Hegel's point is not theirs. In my view he is suggesting a type of demythologizing of the symbols of Incarnation, death, and resurrection, not an elimination of the divine altogether, a demythologizing by which the communal character and universality of these symbols can be realized. The faith of the religious community is not invalidated by the concrete content of pictorial thinking, but it must continually struggle to overcome it. The abstract external divine being needs to be overcome in favor of the inward subjective realization of Spirit. Hegel is not the first religious thinker to make this point. Martin Luther is one of the best examples that comes to mind.[15]

The *Phenomenology of Spirit* is notoriously difficult to interpret. Nevertheless, a reading of the two recent works on the Christology of Hegel by Hans Küng and James Yerkes bears out the interpretation presented in this book.

According to Yerkes, Hegel "developed his system with a clear acknowledgment of the fact that it was in connection with the central symbols of the Christian witness of faith, and particularly that of Incarnation." Incarnation formed the "speculative central point" of Hegel's philosophy. The same is true for Küng.[16] This section on revealed religion shows the deep and lasting impression made on Hegel by the religious symbol of divine descent which he translates here into philosophical conceptuality.[17] Thus he brings this profound and central insight of the Christian tradition into prominent philosophical awareness for the first time.

Due to Hegel's influence, theological discussion of the question of divine mutability and passibility began in Germany with

---

[15] Yerkes understands the relationship of Hegel to religious mythology differently, but this is probably only a terminological difference. See *Christology*, 123, especially n. 50.

[16] Ibid., 3. Küng attempts to connect Hegel to the christological tradition especially in various excursi at the end of his book, *Incarnation of God* (New York: Crossroads, 1987).

[17] See also Hegel's view on incarnation in one of his later Berlin lectures on the philosophy of religion, edited and translated by Peter Hodgson, *The Christian Religion* (Missoula, Mont.: Scholars Press, 1979), 169–221.

an essay in the mid-nineteenth century by I. A. Dorner.[18] Dorner argued that the doctrine of God's immutability expressed absolute ethical self-identity through time, but came to be misunderstood deistically and acosmically. He believed that the Reformation "bore the seeds of a new doctrine" of God's livingness and presence, although it did not create one.[19]

The issue begins to be taken seriously in Britain in the 1920s. Baron von Hügel wrote a response to the fourth edition of James Hinton's *The Mystery of Pain* published in 1870 criticizing Hinton for attributing suffering to God.[20] Von Hügel cited several others who held this view before 1921 and also responded to them. Essentially he argued that God can sympathize with us but cannot suffer because suffering is evil, and God cannot participate in evil.

> Sympathy, yes, indeed, overflowing Sympathy—a Sympathy which we cannot succeed in picturing vividly without drawing upon our own experience of ourselves, where sympathy and suffering are so closely intertwined; but no Suffering in God.[21]

The discussion of the question of God's suffering prompted a classic study published in 1926 commissioned by the Anglican Church, J. K. Mozeley's *The Impassibility of God: A Survey of Christian Thought.*[22] Two years later Bertrand R. Brasnett's *The*

---

[18] "Über die richtige Fassung des dogmatischen Begriffs der Unveränderlichkeit Gottes, mit besonderer Beziehung auf das gegenseitige Verhältnis zwischen Gottes übergeschichtlichen und geschichtlichen Leben, *Jahrbücher für Deutsche Theologie* 1, no.2 (1856): 440ff; 3, no. 4 (1858): 479ff. The third part of this three-part essay was rescued from obscurity and translated into English by Claude Welche, ed., *God and Incarnation in Mid-Nineteenth Century German Theology* (New York: Oxford, 1965), 115–180.

[19] Ibid., 108. See also Robert F. Brown, "Schelling and Dorner and Divine Immutability," *Journal of the American Academy of Religion* 53, no.2 (June 1985), 237–49; Robert R. Williams, "I. A. Dorner: The Ethical Immutability of God," ibid., 54, no.4 (Winter 1986), 721–38.

[20] Baron Von Hügel, "Suffering and God," *Essays and Addresses on the Philosophy of Religion* (London: J. M. Dent, 1921), 167–213.

[21] Ibid., 205; 198.

[22] (Cambridge: University Press, 1926).

Suffering of the Impassible God supported the notion of divine suffering against von Hügel and others.[23]

There were also numerous other works in English in the 1930s and '40s supporting the idea of divine suffering in passing. For H. W. Robinson, for example, "there is no valid philosophical or theological objection against the doctrine that God suffers and . . . the genuinely Christian conception of God requires that, in some sense, He should be a suffering God."[24] Leonard Hodgson's *The Doctrine of the Trinity* contains a description of divine self-limitation as it applies to the Father and the Logos, which comes from the creation of free creatures.

> The eternal Son . . . shares with the Father in that limitation of divine *apatheia* which is involved in the activity of creation. But . . . the Father and the Son know what they are doing. It is part of the divine omniscience to know in detail its own limitations, and that intuitively.[25]

For W. R. Matthews, the atonement implied divine suffering even though it was not the "predominant note in the life of God." The cross is "a sacrament of the life of God . . . I do not see otherwise how we can present any doctrine of the atonement which does justice to the New Testament experience."[26]

Theological writing on divine suffering, emotion, and change continues. The list of theologians who are concerned about this issue is long, and the books and articles of uneven quality. One of the most interesting contemporary books on divine suffering is Werner Elert's *Der Ausgang der altkirchlichen Christologie.*[27] Elert

---

[23] (New York: Macmillan, 1928), 115–50.

[24] *Suffering, Human and Divine* (New York: Macmillan, 1939). Also O. Quick, *Doctrine of the Creed* (New York: Scribner, 1941), 184–87.

[25] (New York: Charles Scribner's Sons, 1944), 77.

[26] *God in Christian Thought and Experience* (London: Nisbet, 1947), 248. Also T. H. Hughes, *The Atonement* (London: Allen and Unwin, 1949), 318. A brief article alerted me to this literature: Richard Bauckham, "Only the Suffering God Can Help: Divine Passibility in Modern Theology," *Themelios* 9, no.3 (April 1984): 6–12.

[27] W. Elert, *Der Ausgang der altkirchlichen Christologie* (Berlin: Lutherisches Verlagshaus, 1957).

had little patience with the problems of inconsistency in the tradition created by the adoption of Greek metaphysics. In regard to the inability of Athanasius to reconcile the becoming flesh of the Word with divine immutability, he states harshly: "Incarnation in the strict sense must imply change. This was the ruin of the entire Athanasian theology."[28] He also argues that the development of Christology necessitated the end of classical metaphysics. He does not mean Chalcedonian Christology, however, which merely rationalized by using it. The coming of God as the infinity of the divine being made every compromise with classical metaphysics impossible. Now there can only be a metaphysics of history developed on christological ground.[29]

Elert thinks that Hilary of Poitiers knew the *Ad Theopompum* and gives various textual parallels to support that thesis. He also believes that the two-natures thinking of Antioch is clearly related to Tertullian. In neither case is he convincing.[30] At the end of his chapter 2, which surveys the idea of the suffering God in Christ up to Justinian, Elert suggests that Justinian's triumphalist Christology in which Jesus is the *despotēs* of the world represses the theopaschite image in which God dies for us. This has definite church-political consequences. The question we need to ask is, is this analysis historically apt or merely an anti-authoritarian critique superimposed on history?

Another work of interest is by Joseph C. McLelland. He writes concerning Clement of Alexandria and Origen:

> What they intended to make clear was that both anthropomorphism and anthropopathism are verbal symbols, improprieties of language, related to divine *paideia*. As apostles of the divine blessedness and perfection, they chose weapons of immutability and impassibility. But their defence created its own mythology of divine ineffability and human theosis which slanted the Gospel toward that perennial philosophy which could but demythologize its historicity.

---

[28] Ibid., 43.
[29] Ibid., 59–66.
[30] Ibid., 83; 79.

He excuses them for this demythologizing because without it
they would have had to reject their philosophical world view.
We, however, are "to blame if we prove unable to follow the
leading of alternative models of the divine."[31] McLelland suggests that classical theism eroded because of its own inner development into Deism: "The rival philosophies of modern Europe,
rationalism and empiricism, are . . . 'philosophies of revolt'
against theism. . . . They reflect the logical extension of the
deus absolutus and his remoteness from the created order—from
'reality!'"[32]

WHITEHEAD

Whitehead made many negative remarks about Christianity,
Christian theology, and some aspects of religion in general.
Lucien Price reports that for eight years during his time in Cambridge, "he was reading theology. This was all extracurricular,
but so thorough that he amassed a sizable theological library. At
the expiry of these eight years he dismissed the subject and sold
the books."[33] He thought of Christian theology as "one of the
great disasters of the human race."[34] "It would be impossible to
imagine anything more un-Christlike than Christian theology."[35]
Whitehead does not blame Jesus for this, but the interpreters of
Christianity, especially Paul. He and Augustine are responsible
for the retreat from the Greek ideals of freedom and "horror of
brutality" to the older Semitic notion of God.

> The old ferocious God is back, the Oriental despot, the Pharoh,
> the Hitler; with everything to enforce obedience, from infant

---

[31] *God the Anonymous: A Study in Alexandrian Philosophical Theology* (Cambridge, Mass.: Philadelphia Patristic Foundation, 1976), 157.
[32] Ibid., 164.
[33] Lucien Price, *Dialogues of Alfred North Whitehead* (New York: Mentor,
1954), 13.
[34] Ibid., 143.
[35] Ibid., 247.

damnation to eternal punishment. In Augustine you get admirable ideas, he is full of light; then you enquire into the ultimate bases of the doctrines and you find this abyss of horror.[36]

In his first lecture on the philosophy of religion from February 1926, Whitehead defined religion as "what the individual does with his own solitariness." In contrast to "collective enthusiasms, revivals, institutions, churches, rituals, bibles, codes of behaviour," which are "the trappings of religion, its passing forms," the heart of religion has to do with "the aweful ultimate fact, which is the human being, consciously alone with itself, for its own sake." The trappings may be "useful, or harmful. . . . But the end of religion is beyond all this."[37]

In the course of his philosophical writings, Whitehead effected a major transformation of the Western understanding of God, one which has been attractive to and debated by philosophers and theologians ever since that time. Although his view is not without several problems, even major ones, it continues to be the most coherent attempt available to include mutability and passibility in a description of God's relation to the world without compromising divine perfection.

Whitehead proposed his view in three major works, *Science and the Modern World, Religion in the Making,* and above all, *Process and Reality.* In the first work he suggests that Aristotle's Prime Mover be replaced by what he called a divine Principle of Concretion.[38] God explains why actual entities, which are the ultimate units of concrete reality, are limited to become the actual thing that each becomes. This limitation is not an act of the divine will as such, but represents three antecedent forms of limitation to which every new entity is subject:

(i) the special logical relations which all events must conform to,
(ii) the selection of relationships to which the events do conform,

---

[36] Ibid., 144–45.
[37] A. N. Whitehead, *Religion in the Making* (New York: World Publishing Co., 1960), 16–17.
[38] A. N. Whitehead, *Science and the Modern World* (New York: Free Press, 1957), 174.

and (iii) the particularity which infects the course even within those general relationships of logic and causation.[39]

Limitation also refers to the fact that every actual entity represents a restriction of possibility, and Whitehead calls this a "second way" in which it occurs.[40] Thus God as the principle of concretion or of limitation ultimately explains why limitation is the price for things becoming real. God is the ultimate ground of order in a world of becoming, and no reason can be given for the divine existence. The existence of God is "the ultimate irrationality."[41]

There is something else at work in this chapter, however, which is not divine, but ultimate in another sense, which Whitehead calls "substantial activity." This will be called creativity by the time of *Religion in the Making* and here already refers to an element to which the Principle of Concretion, like all actual entities, is subject. Whitehead consciously distinguishes this substantial activity from God, fully realizing what he is doing because he mentions the alternative. If we reject the principle of limitation, "we must provide a ground for limitation which stands among the attributes of the substantial activity."[42] The main reason for the distinction between the principle of limitation and substantial activity seems to be that for Whitehead, God is ultimately responsible for evil if they are the same. God

> has been conceived as the foundation of the metaphysical situation with its ultimate activity. If this conception is adhered to, there can be no alternative except to discern in Him the origin of all evil as well as of all good. He is then the supreme author of the play, and to Him must therefore be ascribed its shortcomings as well as its success.[43]

In *Religion in the Making* Whitehead discusses the teaching of Jesus in terms of a new awareness of the divine immanence.

---

[39] Ibid., 177.
[40] Ibid., 178.
[41] Ibid.
[42] Ibid.
[43] Ibid., 179.

The first point is the association of God with the Kingdom of Heaven coupled with the explanation that "The Kingdom of Heaven is within you." The second point is the concept of God under the metaphor of a Father. The implications of this latter notion are expanded with moving insistence in the two Epistles by St. John. . . . To him we owe the phrase, "God is love."[44]

He thinks that Jesus or at least Christianity represented "a serious divergence from the Semitic concept" of God as external and transcendent. Eventually, Whitehead felt, the church returned to the Semitic understanding and added a threefold personality to God.

The metaphysical description in *Religion in the Making* involves three formative elements, creativity, the realm of forms, and the nontemporal actual entity which determines how the forms are ordered, God. Creativity is the new term for substantial activity.[45] The forms or ideas are familiar enough. They are from Plato's theory. God orders these forms, arranging them in hierarchies. Even though God must somehow enter into the constitution of every temporal actual entity, Whitehead is concerned to maintain the eternity and immutability of this divine actual entity.[46] The ending of this book, however, uses images that suggest otherwise. Besides the aspect of the divine nature which "is the complete conceptual realization of the realm of ideal forms," God is also "the ideal companion who transmutes what has been lost into a living fact with his own nature. He is the mirror that discloses to every creature its own greatness."[47] The evil in the world is overcome by good because it enters into and is transmuted by the nature of God, then returned to the world as good. Thus

God has in his nature the knowledge of evil, of pain, and of degradation, but it is there as overcome with what is good. Every fact is what it is, a fact of pleasure, of joy, of pain or of suffering. In its union with God that fact is not a total loss, but on its finer side is an

---

[44] *Religion,* 70.
[45] Ibid., 88.
[46] Ibid., 95.
[47] Ibid., 148.

element to be woven immortally into the rhythm of mortal things. Its very evil becomes a stepping stone in the all embracing ideals of God.[48]

God sustains the world as its antecedent ideal but also provides the "ideal consequent as a factor saving the world from the self-destruction of evil." The page ends with the following statement: *"The world lives by its incarnation of God in itself."* This theme will receive fuller, yet still incomplete exposition at the end of *Process and Reality* where God is "the great companion—the fellow sufferer who understands."[49] To be such a companion and fellow sufferer, God must be mutable and passible in some way.

Whitehead's completed system of metaphysics appears in the Gifford lectures of 1927–28 given in Edinburgh, published as *Process and Reality.* God is an eternal actual entity with the same two poles or natures as every other entity, the primordial or mental, and the consequent or physical. The primordial nature is the complete divine "envisagement" of all the eternal objects, the unchanging evaluation of how things are in the abstract. This is the antecedent source of order and permanence in the world, and from it all temporal entities derive an initial aim toward what they should become.

On the physical or consequent side, God receives all from the world of change, shares or inherits everything which occurs. Temporal entities inherit their limited pasts from those concrete past entities which precede them; God inherits the totality of past entities. They become the divine experience of the temporal world and are woven together with the conceptual experience of eternal objects which precede concrete experience.

The same distinction applies between God and creativity however which we saw in Whitehead's previous works. It is "that ultimate notion of the highest generality at the base of actuality. It cannot be characterized, because all characters are more special than itself." God is "at once a creature of creativity and a

---

[48] Ibid., 149.
[49] A. N. Whitehead, *Process and Reality,* Corrected Edition, (New York: Free Press, 1979), 351.

condition for creativity."[50] God is also called a "primordial, non-temporal accident" of creativity.[51] Creativity is

> the universal of universals characterizing ultimate matter of fact. It is that ultimate principle by which the many, which are the universe disjunctively, become the one actual occasion, which is the universe conjunctively. Creativity is the principle of novelty.[52]

Process and Reality contains Whitehead's last and most important systematic reflections on the nature of God, primordial and consequent, and the relation between God and the world. When seen as primordial, God

> is the unlimited conceptual realization of the absolute wealth of potentiality. In this respect, he is not *before* all creation, but *with* all creation. But, as primordial, so far is he from "eminent reality," that in this abstraction he is "deficiently actual."[53]

The deficiency in the divine primordial nature results from the fact that it is only conceptual, thus not fully actual. Also the conceptual prehensions of God are not conscious unless they are integrated with physical feelings consequent upon the temporal world. There is another side to God's nature "which cannot be omitted."[54]

The consequent nature of God "is the weaving of God's physical feelings upon his primordial concepts." It "originates with physical experience derived from the temporal world, and then acquires integration with the primordial side." Whitehead describes this nature as "determined, incomplete, consequent,

---

[50] Ibid., 31.

[51] Ibid., 7.

[52] Ibid., 21. Several authors object to the subordination of God to creativity in Whitehead for various reasons. It seems essential to maintain it because of the question of evil and God's responsibility for it. If Whitehead is correct here, he has resolved this age-old question which, without his help, remains unsolved. See Robert C. Neville, *Creativity and God: A Challenge to Process Theology* (New York: Seabury, 1980).

[53] *Process and Reality,* 343.

[54] Ibid., 344.

"everlasting," fully actual, and conscious" while God's other nature is "free, complete, primordial, eternal, actually deficient, and unconscious."[55] Through the consequent nature God prehends the world entirely, "its sufferings, its failures, its triumphs, its immediacies of joy" and weaves these into the conceptual scheme. It is the divine judgment on the world. God "saves the world as it passes into the immediacy of his own life. It is the judgment of a wisdom which uses what in the temporal world is mere wreckage."[56]

Whitehead concludes by writing of more than the divine experience of the world, however. He describes how that experience and transformation passes back to it, and thus aids in the overcoming of evil. These are some of the most hopeful pages ever written by a religious thinker. They present a rational explanation for how God's temporal activities improve things, without appealing to miraculous transformations by arbitrary divine *fiat.*

There are four creative phases "in which the universe accomplishes its actuality." First, there is the conceptual origination phase, the divine primordial envisagement of the eternal objects. Next, the temporal actualities come individually into existence determined to some extent by the first phase which lays down the antecedent conditions for their existence, ultimately giving them their aim. This phase accounts for the actual existence of actual things. Third, "there is the phase of perfected actuality, in which the many are one everlastingly, without the qualification of any loss either of individual identity or of completeness of unity." Here God prehends the actual world, and comprehends it in weaving together the actualities with relevant envisaged possibilities. Finally in the last phase,

> Creative action completes itself. For the perfected actuality passes back into the temporal world, and qualifies this world so that each temporal actuality includes it as an immediate fact of relevant experience. For the kingdom of heaven is with us today.

---

[55] Ibid., 345.
[56] Ibid., 346.

This is "the love of God for the world. It is the particular providence for particular occasions. What is done in the world is transformed into a reality in heaven, and the reality in heaven passes back into the world." In other words God's temporal activity is the reception of all that happens, its transformation according to the divine primordial vision, then passing back this improved reality to future entities in the world of becoming. "By reason of this reciprocal relation, the love in the world passes into the love in heaven, and floods back again into the world. In this sense, God is the great companion—the fellow-sufferer who understands."[57]

No matter how one attempts to reconcile this powerful image of the unity of the divine with the cosmic and human with Whitehead's two natures of God, the image itself is primary and ought not to be set aside. The grounds for hope in the world of good and evil is that the great companion is constantly working for improvement by offering relevant possibilities for overcoming evil, because the evil has already been overcome on the divine level. Several examples might be given on the human level where this miracle occurs almost daily. Divine suggestions of relevant possibilities for personal healings, for work-related creativity, and for overcoming poverty, ignorance, and war abound in the world, and we seldom take advantage of them. Two examples on the natural level, however, will bear this out.

First, there is the case of a small lake in a heavily populated suburb. A busy superhighway literally cuts it in half. Automobiles pour exhaust smoke into the air there twenty-four hours a day. Since the lake is so easily available, several residents like to run their power launches back and forth on the lake and even water-ski on the deeper half. Amazingly enough, however, this small lake is also heavily populated with ducks, who seem not to mind the automobile and boat traffic, but serenely raise their young, quacking happily amid the racket of modern machinery. Hawks, muskrats, and bass live there, as well. Nature has

[57] Ibid., 350–51.

adjusted to modern life, at least in this small region, and its
evils have been overcome, at least for the present.

Second, there is the example of the bird nest constructed totally out of old fishing line, one of the new plastic types that is
almost indestructible, at least by natural means. Some bird sensed
the relevant possibility of this potential evil and now has a nest
which is far superior to those made of grass, leaves, and sticks.

No great theistic proof can be launched from these homely
examples, but they bring out concretely how God acts in the world
in small yet surprising ways. The great companion and fellow-
sufferer tends the earth that we neglect, as well as the human race
whose doings even now remain somewhat mysterious to us. This
is ultimately the meaning of the Incarnation.

Some in the tradition attempted to align their attachment to
the God of Scripture and to belief in the Incarnation with their
philosophical commitment to divine immutability and impassibility. Several important texts deal with the Scriptural passages
about divine repentance, wrath, and jealousy, and those that
realistically portray God's love and mercy. Philo of Alexandria is
often characterized as a religious thinker who totally absorbed
Greek philosophy at the expense of the Biblical understanding
of God. The fact that, in spite of good philosophical precedent,
he never describes God as *apathēs* or *analloiōtos* even once in his
entire corpus is significant. This, when combined with a careful
reading of his text on immutability, indicates that the God of
Philo is not the God of Plato, at least, not entirely.

Justin the Apologist absorbs the Middle Platonic view of
God fairly completely, but not totally. He is also quite biblical,
not really understanding the possible inconsistency. Justin simply used philosophical tools that were readily available in order
to defend and explain the Christian belief in God. He was incapable of transforming them.

No Christian writers internalized the prevailing view of God
more than the Alexandrians. Those few texts in which Clement
describes God as passible are signs that at times he too sensed its
inadequacy. Consider Origen's homily attributing passibility to
the Father and Son. One can debate the significance of any one

text. Yet one can argue that in Origen, the unique Christian understanding of God began to influence philosophical reflection. The *Ad Theopompum* certainly shows this because it focuses the problem clearly for the first time. In the growing awareness of Christianity and theology, the issue of divine suffering and change eventually centers on Jesus, the divine Incarnate Word.

In response to the Arian argument about change Athanasius saw what was at stake. Although he holds to divine immutability axiomatically, as all did in the fourth century, nevertheless, in Jesus, God suffered. This is no paradox, but a new vision of God needing an appropriate philosophical justification. Although Athanasius did not formulate this justification successfully because of philosophical limitation, this does not invalidate his theology as Elert thought. His treatise on the Incarnation is the first attempt to center attention on Jesus as God's divine Word.

Even though he does not apply his insight to the divine level, Gregory of Nyssa's positive view of change on the human level and his occasional teaching that human emotions are good, opens the way for a new understanding of Christian anthropology. This does have some effect on his christological statements also. The *Commentary on the Psalms* from Tura is a fourth-century text which offers a viable philosophical term for divine mutability in the Incarnation, one that preserves its religious truth as well as rationality. The author, drawing from Aristotle, distinguishes among various types of change, and suggests that one type truly did take place in the Incarnation.

Latin writers, beginning with Tertullian, confronted the question, but less successfully. Tertullian recognizes that the biblical understanding of divine emotion and change needs to be preserved and may even be used to correct philosophy. His suggestions are radical and creative, arguing as he does that God must have emotions and must change in order to be perfect. Nevertheless Tertullian does not systematize these intuitions because his intention is nearly always polemic.

Lactantius argues after him that God should appropriately feel anger, something strenuously denied by his own teacher Arnobius. The *de ira dei* develops a logic for divine emotions which seems to die with the author. Lactantius's treatise influences neither Hilary nor Augustine, yet they do show the new awareness which came from Athanasius, that the Incarnation of the divine Word is at the heart of Christian faith. Neither of them recast the idea of divine immutability and impassibility. It is not until modern times that the full significance of the belief in divine incarnation is grasped on the philosophical level, principally by Hegel and Whitehead, even though such may not have been their conscious intention. Obviously their theologies are far from perfect and need further study and development. Yet one cannot help but believe, if one is a Christian, that the very development of better ways to experience and to conceptualize the nearness of the divine originates with the great companion who assumed the form of a slave.

INDEX